IMAGES
of America

ANDERSON VALLEY

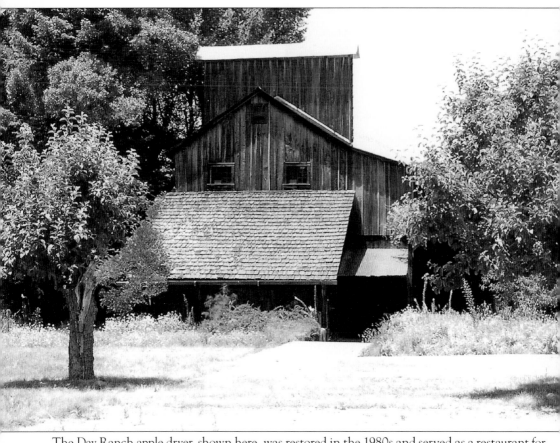

The Day Ranch apple dryer, shown here, was restored in the 1980s and served as a restaurant for a few years. One of the original dryers in the valley, it now provides the perfect setting to show off the beauty of the valley.

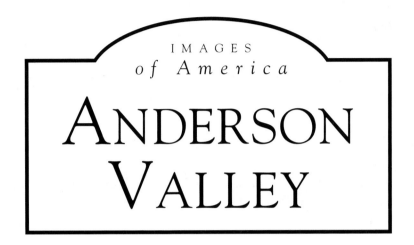

IMAGES
of America

ANDERSON
VALLEY

Anderson Valley Historical Society

Copyright © 2005 by Anderson Valley Historical Society
ISBN 0-7385-3017-4

Published by Arcadia Publishing
Charleston SC, Chicago IL, Portsmouth NH, San Francisco CA

Printed in Great Britain

Library of Congress Catalog Card Number: 2005928934

For all general information contact Arcadia Publishing at:
Telephone 843-853-2070
Fax 843-853-0044
E-mail sales@arcadiapublishing.com
For customer service and orders:
Toll-Free 1-888-313-2665

Visit us on the internet at http://www.arcadiapublishing.com

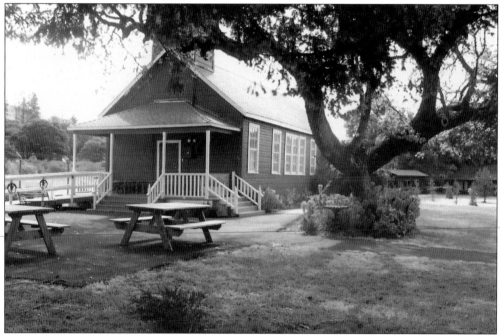

Con Creek School, built in 1891, was an eight-grade, one-room school until 1941. Between 1941 and 1958, it met a variety of school needs. From 1958 to 1979, it was "The Kindergarten." In 1979, its doors closed. Almost 90 years after the first children moved in, the last kindergarten class graduated. That same year, the valley rallied around saving this important landmark. Con Creek School, located at 12340 Highway 128 in Boonville, functions today as our beloved museum.

CONTENTS

ACKNOWLEDGMENTS

We have many to thank for these photographs of life in Anderson Valley during the 19th and 20th centuries. We must begin by acknowledging Robert Lee. His wonderful private collection not only provided us with seven binders of incredible photographs, but each image included a caption. This collection sparked an incredible energy in our team and made the completion of this project much simpler. Those who were kind enough to share photographs from their personal collections include Eileen Pronsolino, Donald Pardini, Pat Hulbert, Joyce Lowrey Christen, Hayes Brennan, Wilma Brink, Shorty Adams, Roederer Estate, Katherine Nobels Sinnott, Wesley Smoot, Bo and Bobbie Hiatt, Charmian Blattner, Vern and Marilyn Ornbaun, Rodger Tolman, Sharolyn Bierman, Vicky Center, Joann Borges, Christine Clark, Shine and Beth Tuttle, Ava Glover, Ken and Kim Allen, Zac Robinson, Mary Beth Chandler, and Alan Green. The remaining photos came from the collection of the Anderson Valley Historical Society.

We must also thank those who took the time to share their memories. It is our good fortune that there are descendents from those earlier times still living in the valley. What fun it has been to hear their stories. The books and files at the museum also contain wonderful stories and memories, written by those who throughout the years have taken a moment to "write it down." We are especially grateful to them. What a pleasure it is for us to share these memories of Anderson Valley.

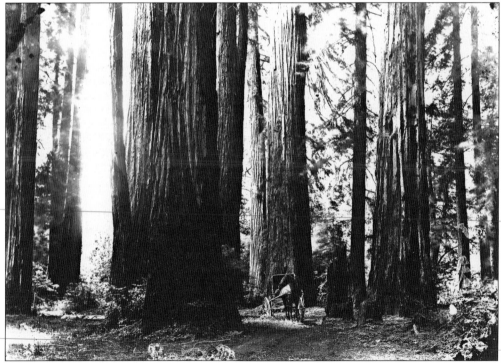

These gigantic redwood trees can be seen in the groves of Hendy Woods. The grove was first claimed by Joshua Hendy in the late 1800s and he declared that no man would ever take an ax to it. Following his death, logging did occur on some lands, but his grove was spared. In August 1958, these lands were purchased by the State of California, becoming Hendy Woods State Park.

INTRODUCTION

Beautiful Anderson Valley lies in southwestern Mendocino County. It is nestled in the coastal range, less than an hour from the Pacific Ocean. The area we call Anderson Valley begins near Yorkville and extends just beyond Navarro, a distance of 25 miles. Three major rivers weave through the valley and merge in Philo to form the Navarro River. Rancheria Creek runs from Yorkville, turning away from the valley and into the mountains just south of Boonville, then returning to the valley at Philo. Anderson Creek runs through the valley from Boonville to Philo. Indian Creek begins in the hills above Boonville and runs through the valley at Philo. The valley floor is flanked by high hills. While these rivers and hills create the beauty we all love, they made settlement very difficult. However, the long valley and beautiful redwoods caused Henry and Isaac Beeson and their stepbrother, William Anderson, the first white men to see the valley, to report back to their families that they had found a "big meadow, and it was like a garden of Eden."

The early stewards of this land were Pomo Indians. The Late (Lah-tay) Pomo or Ma-cu-maks lived in the present-day area of Yorkville. Another group, the Tabahtea (Tah-bah-tay) Pomo lived in the Boonville area west to Navarro. There were 19 known village sites, with an estimated population of around 600 in 1855. The four major villages were "Late," on the west bank of Rancheria Creek about one mile west of Yorkville, "Lemkolil," on the northeast bank of Anderson Creek one mile downstream from Boonville, "Tabate," on the northeast bank of the Navarro River two miles west of Philo, and "Katuuli," 50 yards south of the old town of Christine, near the present day Christine Woods.

The first white settlers arrived in 1852. Over the next few years, several settlements were formed in the valley: Christine, Hop Flat, Philo, Peachland, Bell Valley, The Corners/Boonville, Hermitage, and Whitehall. Each of these communities was separate and unique. Christine was settled by seven families who were originally from a small village in the Swiss Alps. Hop Flat was a small logging community, so named because of the numerous dances held there. Hop Flatters feet wouldn't stand still—they hopped around all night. Bell Valley was a hop-growing region made famous by Boontling, the strange local language that began there. The Corners/Boonville was a commercial center. Hermitage and Whitehall were stage stops. In addition to the tasks of settlement, valley people took up sheep ranching, planted apple orchards and hop fields, and began logging operations. Because of the distance covered by the valley, flanking hills, and mountains, each community had its own schools, stores, and churches.

During the early 1900s, Anderson Valley was bustling. On the western end of the valley a new community arose called Wendling. A railroad was built between that area and the coast. The railroad hauled lumber, people, and supplies to provide an important link between San Francisco and this area of rich natural resources. Tan oak harvesting became an important part of the economy. Italian immigrants settled in the Greenwood area, planting vineyards. Those that raised apple orchards found they did very well in the valley soils and climate, thus the orchards expanded. One of the early stage stop areas grew to become Yorkville. Roads were built, including MacDonald to the Sea, the Ukiah Toll Road, and Navarro Ridge Road, connecting the valley to the outside world. Tourists from San Francisco trekked to Anderson Valley to hunt, fish, and get away from the city. The Depression, Prohibition, and war arrived in the 1930s and 1940s. Anderson Valley residents, like everywhere else, found life very difficult during these times.

Then the boom came after World War II, as timber was in great demand, and Anderson Valley had a plentiful supply. Mills sprang up everywhere. At the peak, there were 50 mills in the valley. Another group of immigrants came to the area, this time from Oklahoma and Arkansas, and schools were bursting at their seams. The settlements were long gone, replaced by four commercial centers: Yorkville, Boonville, Philo, and Navarro. The early resorts came back to life, new ones were added, and all were busier than ever. Several very large sheep ranches operated and Anderson Valley apples were known around the world.

In the 1970s, one man's "folly" led to another big change in the valley. Not only did apples like the climate and soils, but grapes did too. Vineyards and eventually wineries began to spring up throughout the valley. With the vineyard growth, another new group of people came to the area, this time from Mexico. Additionally, urban refugees found Anderson Valley life to be a welcome respite from the hustle and bustle of the cities. The one thing that has remained constant through every stage of its history is a love of this beautiful land.

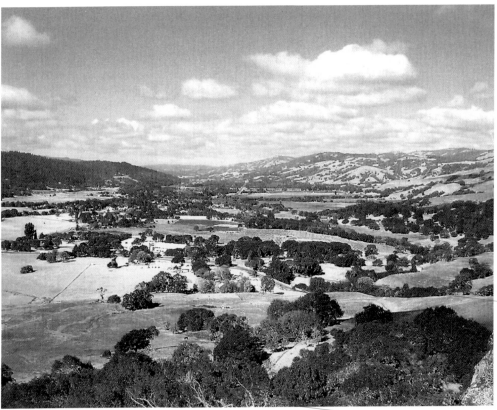

Taken from "Burger Rock" on the Johnson Ranch, this recent photo sets the scene for the pictures and stories of this book. This is approximately the spot from which the first white settlers viewed the valley. The beauty of the valley is as breathtaking today as it was then.

One

OT'N ON THE RANCH

By following one property through the years, it will be seen how Anderson Valley agriculture has both stayed the same as well as changed.

J. T. Farrer purchased his Anderson Valley ranch in 1906. When he made the purchase, the principal income from the property was hops. The ranch had a large hop kiln for drying the product before shipment. Later, when hops were no longer profitable, the Farrers planted the fields into hay and raised livestock. They added a small vineyard and fruit trees, principally prunes, of which there was a sizable orchard. Plums, apples, pears, and walnuts were planted for the enjoyment of the family.

For some years after Farrer's death in 1917, the farm lay idle. His widow left the ranch, returning in the late 1920s with her youngest son Maurice. Upon returning, they planted the fields into alfalfa and developed a herd of Guernsey dairy cows, shipping cream to Petaluma. They raised their own feed, alfalfa, and oats. Sheep grazed the hills on the east side of the ranch. Maurice pulled the prune trees and extended the small apple orchard. By the 1930s, it was no longer feasible to ship cream and the dairy herd was sold.

In 1954, Maurice planted additional apple trees. He continued raising sheep until the coming of the expressway. The thoroughfare split the ranch and they sold the eastern hillsides, which were subsequently subdivided, becoming vineyards and homesteads. Modern Orchards purchased and marketed the western side of the ranch in 1987. Apples were planted using a new technique for the "gourmet" and "health food" markets.

Today the "Farrer Ranch" has an olive orchard, the most recent addition to valley agriculture. There are vineyards as well, reflecting one of the most dramatic changes in the valley. The orchards include Asian pear, cherry, peach trees, and a blueberry patch, perhaps to meet the needs of the gourmet market. And, there are still apple orchards. Thus agriculture has always been, and continues to be, the fabric of Anderson Valley life.

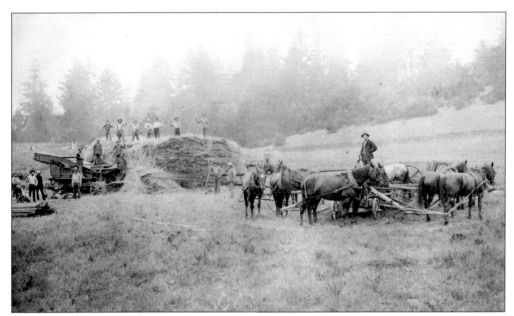

Jim Sanders's thrashing machine cuts down oats and barley, which was powered by six teams of horses who walked in a circle. Ranchers in the area would haul their grain to the thrasher, and then horses would move the device to another location further down the valley. This method was used in the 1880s and 1890s.

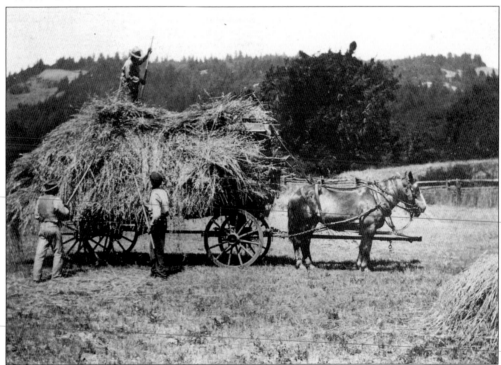

Teams of horses and wagons hauled the hay and grain from the fields to the thrashing machine or to a barn for winter storage. This crew is hauling their load from the Dightman ranch on Indian Creek. William Otis is on the load and George Brown is on the left side on the ground.

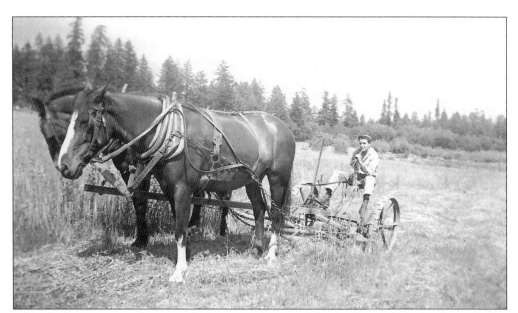

After the hay was mowed, it was raked into windrows and shocked into piles before being hauled to the barn. Here Angelo Pronsolino's horses nibbled on some succulent heads of grain.

As shown in this 1942 photograph of the Dightman Ranch, hayforks were used to put the hay in the hayloft. When the fork opened, it straddled the load. Then, when tension was pulled, the fork would close on a large amount of hay, and by block and tackle, it was lifted to the peak of the barn. The fork ran on a track to the back of the barn, where the load was dropped into the hayloft.

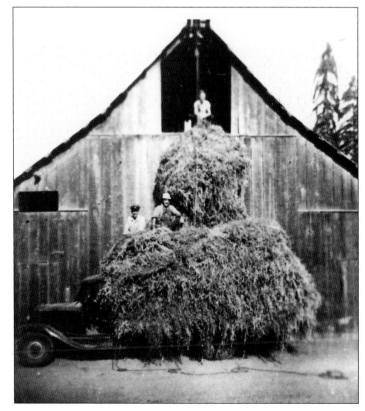

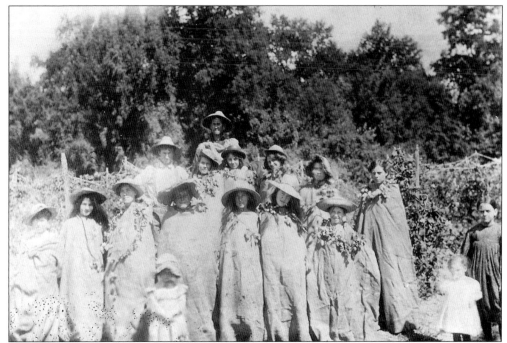

Hops were a primary crop in the late 1800s and early 1900s. These pickers wear burlap to keep the spines on the hop vines from wearing down their clothes. Men, women, and children worked in the fields together.

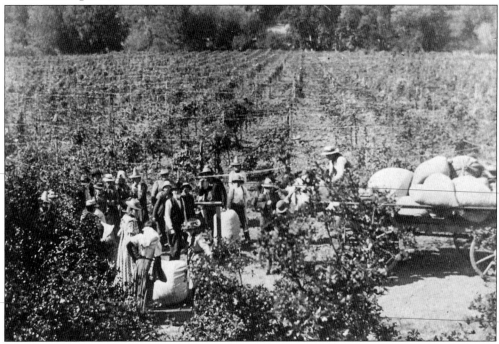

Hop pickers were paid by the pound. At the end of a tiring day, the crew weighed the result from their work in the fields. The bags were then loaded on wagons and hauled to the kiln for drying. Hops were grown in rows on trellises.

Fresh-picked bags of green hops were lifted to the upper part of the drying kiln, where they were dried before being compressed into bales. One might say that the device lifting the bags of hops from the wagons to the upper part of the kiln was an early rendition of the modern-day forklift. This hop kiln was located on the Gowan Ranch west of Philo.

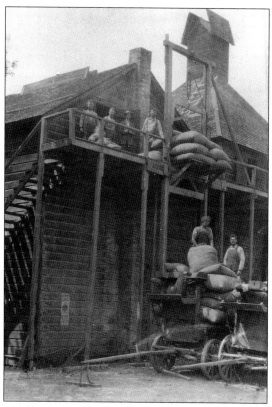

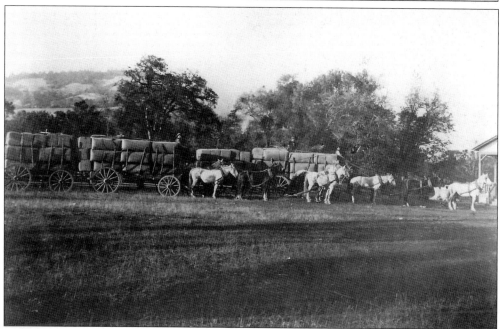

After thoroughly drying, the hops were compressed into bales and encased in burlap bags for shipping to market. Here, two wagons and two wagon trailers are being loaded with bales of hops to be transported to a railhead, which was probably in Cloverdale.

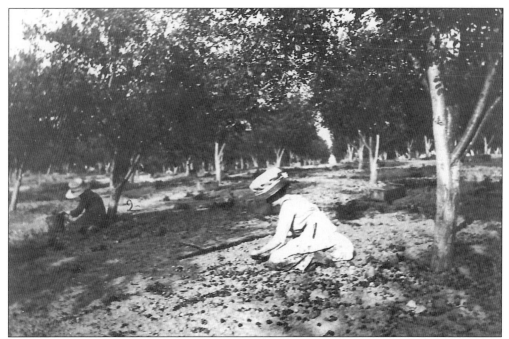

The climate and soils of Anderson Valley have supported a variety of orchards, including prunes. During picking time, even teachers took a turn, as shown in this image of Miss Elliott, a teacher who helped out at the Joel Reilly place. The prunes were shaken off the trees and then picked up from the ground, which was a backbreaking job. For this they were paid 15¢ for a 50-pound lug box.

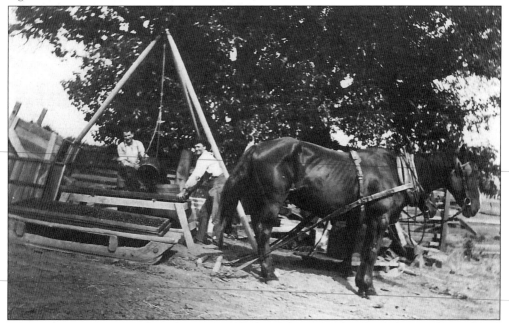

After picking, prunes were dipped into a vat filled with lye water, then loaded onto a horse-drawn sled and taken to an open area for sun drying. The lye solution caused the skin on the prunes to crack open, allowing them to dry more rapidly.

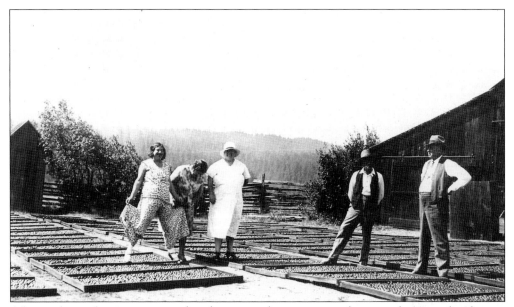

After soaking, the prunes were placed on trays that were spread out on the ground to be sun dried as shown here at the Schoenahl Ranch in Boonville. Myrtis Schoenahl is pictured on the far left and Archie Schoenahl is on the far right.

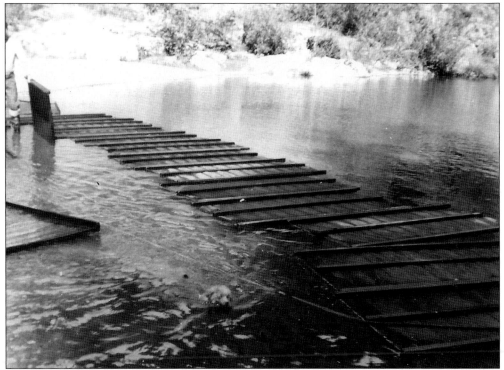

The Hulberts took their trays to the Navarro River and cleaned them in preparation for the next load of prunes. After they soaked the trays to loosen the dried drippings, they used a wire brush to scrub them, as shown in this 1954 image.

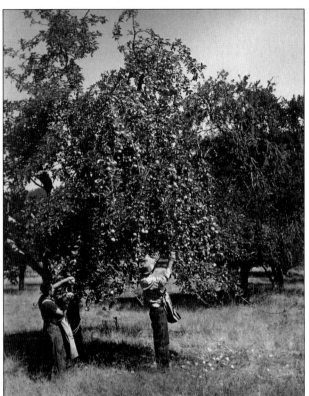

Apples were one of the valley's main industries from the 1930s through the 1960s. At one time, there were 64 orchards growing as many as 90 varieties of apples in Anderson Valley. Today there remains only one large apple orchard and packing shed, owned by the Gowans, descendents of an early valley family. As Bob Glover and Carl Schmidt picked, they put the apples in the bags they wore before dumping them into 50-pound lug boxes.

One of the earlier large apple orchards was owned by Harwood June. Frank Luff and his wife Effie, shown here, worked in June's orchards for many years. Frank was also chief of the Pomo Indian tribe in Southern Mendocino County.

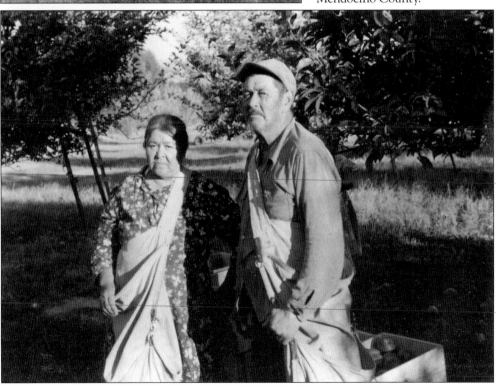

Cecil Gowan carefully arranges boxes of fresh apples and peaches for sale at Gowan's Oak Tree in the mid-1950s. All of the fruit was grown and harvested on the Gowan ranch. Today Cecil's son and grandchildren run the ranch and Gowan's Oak Tree is a popular stop for locals and tourists alike.

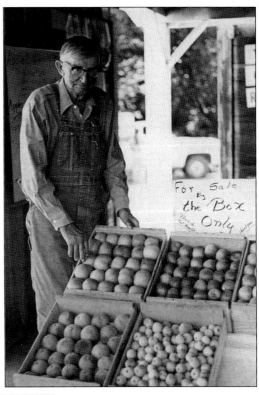

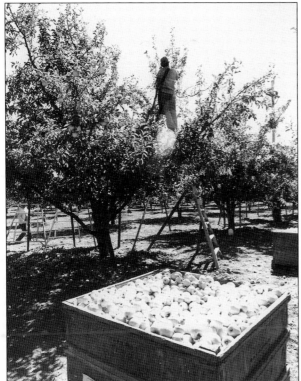

Apples were later picked and placed in bins instead of boxes, as in this 1986 photograph. The larger bins replaced the 50-pound lug box and could be handled by a forklift mounted on a tractor. This cut time and manpower.

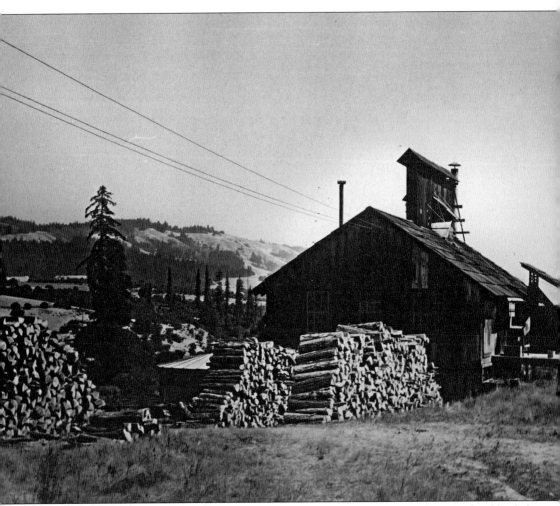

Prior to the 1950s, Anderson Valley was home to 60-plus apple dryers. Apples were dried both for long-term preservation and for ease in shipping. This dryer was located on the Clark Ranch in the Philo area. The early dryers had a boiler that was fired with wood. Cutting firewood to burn in the dryers was a never-ending job. The wood had to be cut to a size that would fit in the boiler.

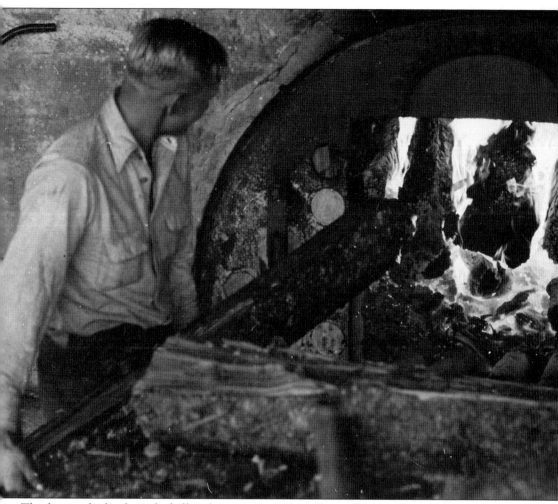

The furnace had to be stoked all night to maintain heat. It usually took about 24 hours to dry a batch of apples. Earl Clark is feeding this furnace on his ranch near Philo.

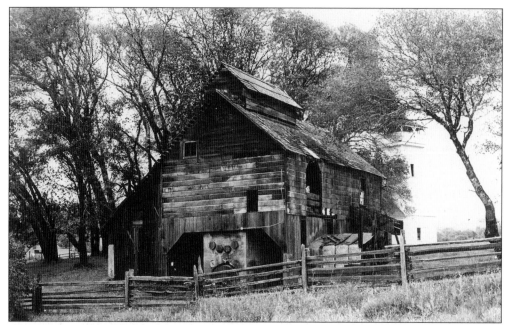

The first apple dryer in Anderson Valley was located on the Guntly Ranch. This view shows the furnace, which supplied heat to dry the apples. The heat, which was supplied by wood in the early days and later by oil, was exhausted through the add-on roof. A large metal pan filled with sulfur was placed above the furnace, which was then ignited. The fumes and smoke from the sulfur gave the apples a nice white color.

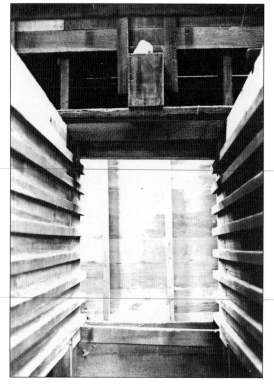

This view shows the rack area of the dryer where the trays filled with peeled, cored, and sliced apples were placed. The heat from the furnace then circulated through the apples. There were many of these rack areas within the dryer.

As the roads and modes of transportation improved, apples were shipped whole. Ranchers began building packing sheds where apples were stored for the fresh fruit market. This truck, loaded with boxes of apples, is headed for a packing shed, probably on the Earl Clark ranch. On this and many other ranches in the valley, vineyards have replaced the apple orchards. Carl Schmidt's horse doesn't seem to know there are apples on the truck.

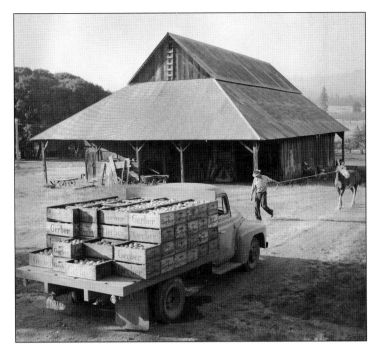

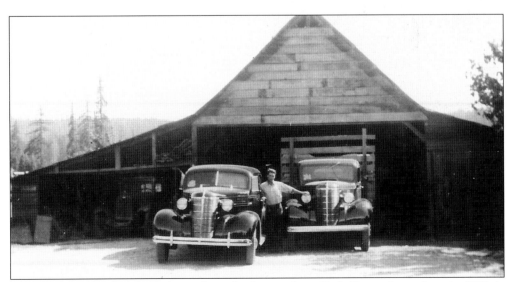

The apples were taken from the packing shed to market. Clyde Price, shown here in 1938, is leaving the packing shed on his ranch in Philo with a load of fruit, which will be delivered to the coast.

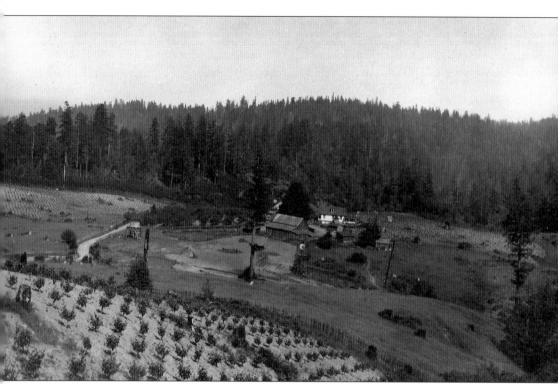

Grapes and wine have been a part of valley agriculture since the late 1800s, when a number of Italian immigrants came to Greenwood from San Francisco. The early settlers included the Valentis, Fratis, Demeterios, Tovanis, Guistis, and Giovanettis. The old Valenti Ranch and Vineyard, believed to be the first in the area, was in Greenwood. Men and horses cleared the land by hand. Most families squeezed their own juice and made their own wine. The Greenwood/Signal Ridge area was known as Vinegar Hill. Some said this originated during Prohibition when people trekked to the ridge for "vinegar." Others said it was because unripe and/or rain- and frost-damaged grapes often went into the wine.

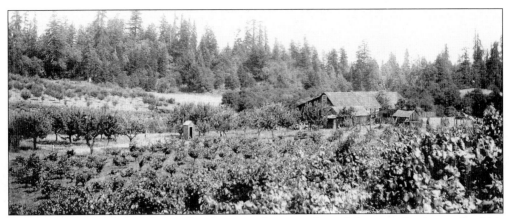

As time went on, those who made a very good wine enlarged their production and sold it commercially. Wineries began purchasing grapes from small ranchers. During the World War I era, there may have been as many as 150 acres of wine grapes growing in the Fish Rock area and more than 200 acres on Greenwood Ridge. Theresa and Johnny Pronsolino moved to Greenwood Ridge in 1923 and planted grapes. This is their vineyard as it looked in the 1930s.

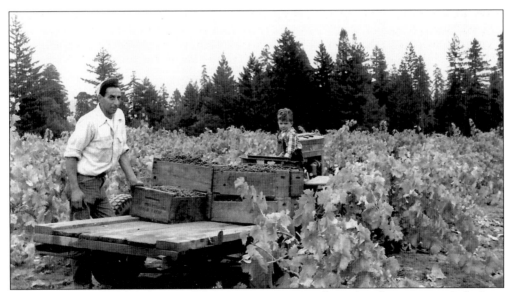

Prohibition, and killer frosts in the 1940s, brought an end to the early valley wine era. Only three of the original old vine vineyards remained. Zeni and Ciapusci Vineyards are still owned by the original Italian families. The Dupratt Vineyard is the third and is approaching its 90th birthday (planted in 1916). Angelo Pronsolino and his son David, shown here in 1951, were harvesting fruit that they sold to the Dupratts.

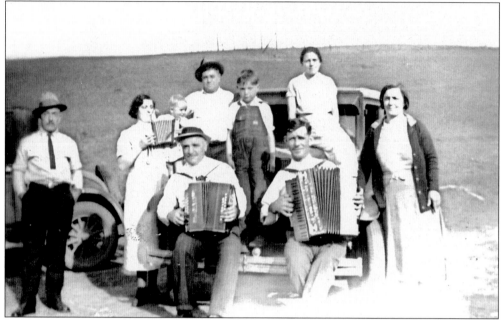

In 1911–1912, Joe Pinoli began planting grapes on sloping hillsides in the Mill and Lazy Creek areas between Philo and Navarro. Jon and Charles Pinoli bought land nearby and began planting in 1917. These vineyards were the first to be established on the valley floor rather than the ridges. Joe Pinoli founded the first bonded winery in the valley. Pictured here, from left to right, are unidentified, John Pinoli, Pete Acquistapacci, Claudina Pinoli, Julia Pinoli, Charley Pinoli, Johnnie, Pinoli, Maria Acquistapacci, and Tarissa Acquistapacci.

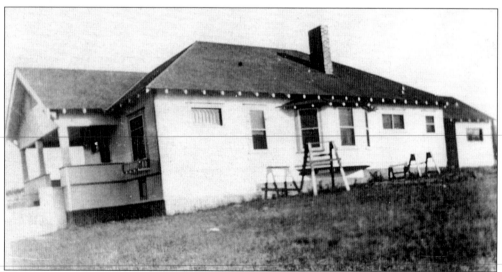

In the late 1960s, Dr. Edmeades, a Southern California physician, planted 24 acres of premium wine grapes and hung up a sign that read, "Edmeades Folly." His "folly" led to changes throughout the valley as ranches changed hands and crops. The Nunn Ranch was sold to Tony and Gretchen Husch. Grapes were planted, and the back room of the Nunn Ranch house, built in 1920, became the first modern winery in 1971.

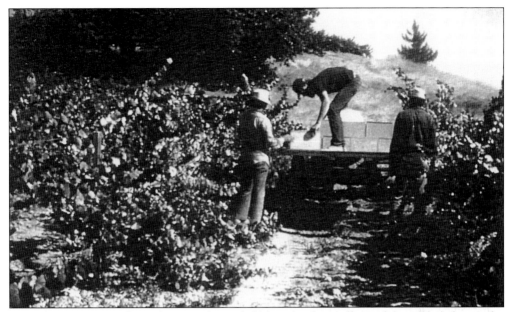

Pinot Noir grapes are being harvested into field lugs (traditionally used for apples) during the 1974 harvest at Husch Vineyards. Tony and Gretchen planted the valley's first Pinot Noir and the success of the planting led others to follow suit. Today Anderson Valley is noted for its premium Pinot Noir wine. In 1979, Hugo Oswald Jr. bought the Husch Winery. Husch Vineyards is owned and operated by the third generation of the Oswald family, Zac Robinson and Amanda Robinson Holstine.

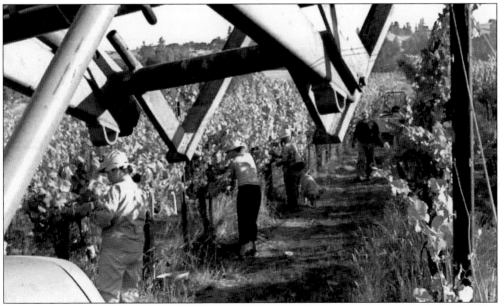

Hans and Thereisa Kobler planted grapes in the late 1960s, returning the Pinoli Ranch of the 1900s to vineyard. Lazy Creek Winery became the valley's second modern, bonded winery in 1973, about 50 years after Joe Pinoli founded the first bonded valley winery on the same ranch. Josh and Mary Beth Chandler purchased Lazy Creek in 1999. Norman Kobler, Hans and Thereisa's son, continues with his own valley vineyard and manages others in the valley.

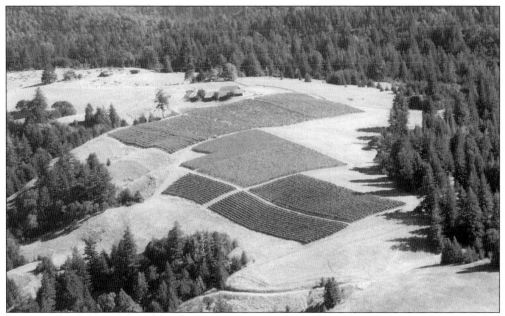

In 1972, Allan Green followed the lead of early Italian settlers and planted eight acres of grapes on Greenwood Ridge. In the 1980s, he built his wine-tasting room on the valley floor. Greenwood Ridge Vineyards continues today as a major contributor to the Anderson Valley premium wine industry.

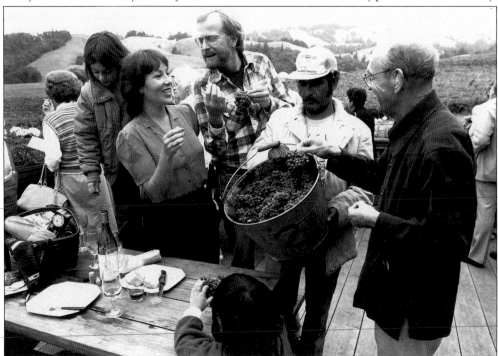

Harvest is always a busy (and fun) time, as shown in this photograph taken during the Navarro Vineyards 1986 yield. Navarro Vineyard owners Ted Bennett and Deborah Cahn have been growing grapes, making award-winning wine, and producing non-alcoholic grape juices in Anderson Valley since 1974.

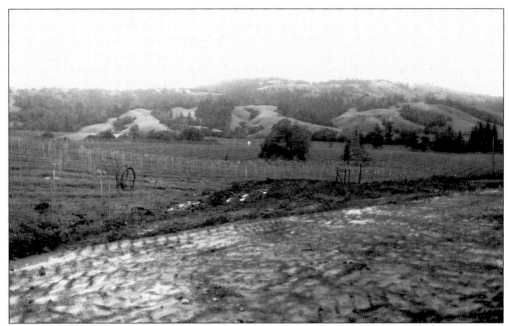

An important moment in Anderson Valley wine history took place in 1981, when the French firm Champagne Louis Roederer announced plans to build a California sparkling wine facility in Anderson Valley. They began planting vines on the valley floor in 1982. The winery officially began operation in 1986, and released 4,500 cases of its first wine, the Anderson Valley Brut, in 1988.

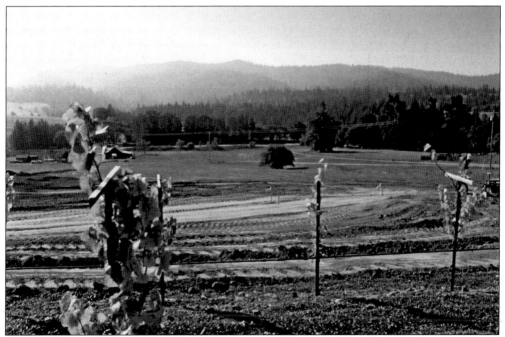

During the 1980s, scenes like this were commonplace, as winery expansion in Anderson Valley continued on a grand scale. Scharfenberger Cellars, Handley Cellars, Christine Woods, Pullman Vineyard, and Pepperwood Springs all began producing wine during these years.

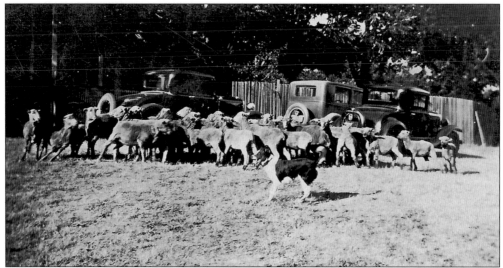

Sheep ranching has always been a mainstay of valley agriculture. At one time there were 75,000 head of sheep grazing the hills of the valley. Sheep dogs are a sheep rancher's most valuable possession. This dog was gathering sheep on Lolly Gossman's ranch in 1938. A local rancher was once asked why he allowed his dog to sleep on the seat of his new pickup. He answered, "My dog paid for my pickup. He can sleep there anytime."

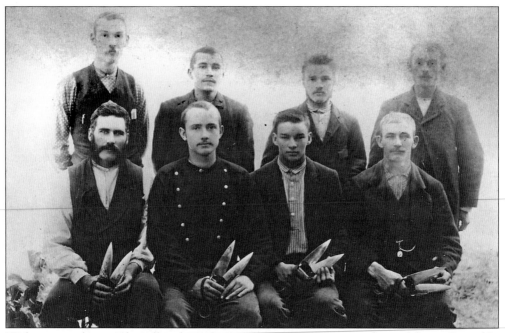

With so many sheep in the valley, sheep shearing became a way to earn a living. Marvin Reynolds, born in 1874, wrote that shearers were paid 4¢ per head. They could clip between 80 and 100 sheep per day. Sheep-shearing crews traveled from ranch to ranch, sleeping in barns. The lady of the ranch cooked for the crews. Pictured in this image from around 1900, from left to right, are John Ward, Ralph Brown, Guy Whipple, Jake Harrison, John L. Prather, Earl Prather, Bert Whipple, and (unknown) Lawson.

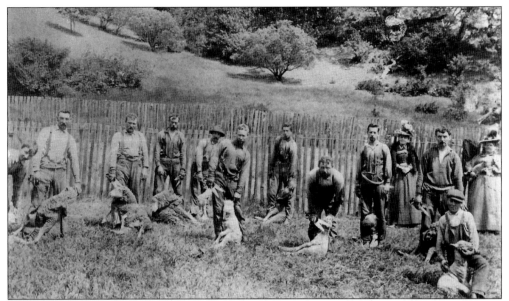

The blades used by these men were as sharp as a surgeon's instruments. It is said that the good shearers from these days could shear as many head per day as later shearers could with shearing machines. This crew was working in Bell Valley. Pictured here, from left to right, are Charley Wallach, John Wallach, Verl Ornbaun, Casey Melville, Poke Wallach, Dick McDonald, "Ivey" Ledford, Bowlen Hiatt, Vick Miller, Mary Hiatt, Frank Wallach, Sid "Dickie" Duff, and Emily Wallach-Miller.

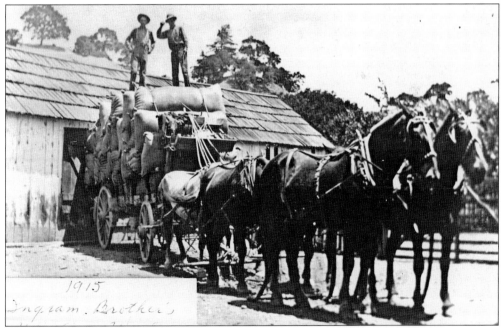

After shearing, the fleece was tied with paper twine, and then placed in a large burlap sack. The wool was tromped down in the sack to get it as full as possible. A full sack of wool would weigh between 300 to 350 pounds. This wagonload of sacked wool is headed to the railhead in Cloverdale. The men on top of the load are Irvin Ingram (left) and Ted Ingram.

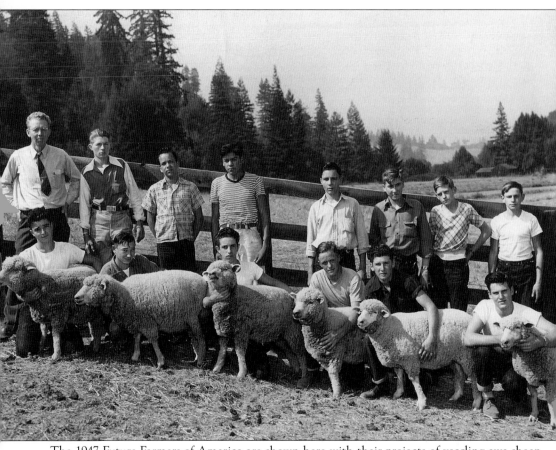

The 1947 Future Farmers of America are shown here with their projects of yearling ewe sheep. Glen Johnson, one of the large sheep ranchers at the time, donated the animals. Pictured, from left to right, are Danny Lawson, Bob Paul, Hoyt Ross, Floyd Johnson, Donald Pardini, Bob Canaveri, Russell Miller (teacher), Neil Sparks, Alvin Jones, Arthur Knight, Wesley Farrell, Clyde Paul, Donald Snow, and Tommy Burger.

Shearing machines came into use in the 1930s; note the electric motors in the upper left. A gear-driven shaft extends from the motor to a hand-held head, which operates much like a pair of barber's clippers. The sling around the shearer's chest is fastened by a rope, which runs up through a pulley to a sack of rocks. This offsets the shearer's weight as he bends over the sheep. These shearers are working on the Austin Hulbert Ranch in 1973.

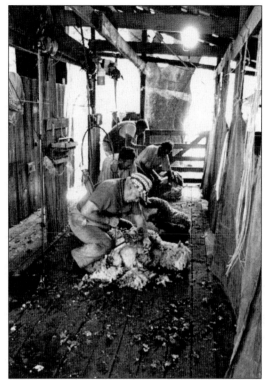

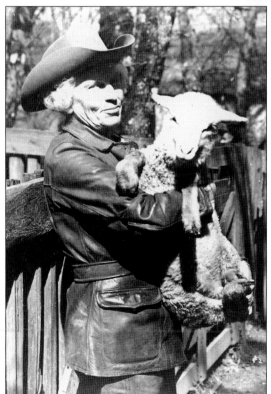

Kate and Ward Mailliard first came to the valley for vacations and later purchased the Ornbaun Ranch. For years the ranch was their country home. In the 1940s, they teamed up with UC Davis to bring Merino sheep to the valley from Australia, raising them for their fine wool. Kate, assisted by ranch manager Guido Pronsolino, worked with Merinos for 29 years. Visitors have long marveled at the Mailliard Redwood Reserve, an old-growth redwood forest the family donated to the state.

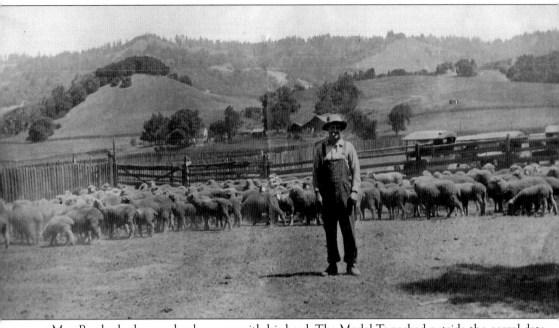

Max Rawles looks proud as he poses with his herd. The Model Ts parked outside the corral date the photograph. Joseph Rawles arrived in the valley in 1857, taking up a claim in the Peachland area. In 1858, he purchased the Walter Anderson home and land. By 1880, he owned 1,600 acres of farming and grazing land, stocked with 3,160 head of sheep.

Two

HARPIN BOONT

Boontling, the language that Anderson Valley is known for, began in the 1880s in the hop fields of Bell Valley, about six miles east of Boonville, and flourished until 1915. There are varying accounts of how it began. Some think the most convincing account states that the women of Bell Valley started the language. In this version, a young woman in the Bay Area became pregnant without the benefit of marriage. To protect her parents from shame, the girl went to live with friends in Bell Valley. Local women worked together in the hop fields, passing the time with conversation. Because the young woman worked among them, they made up words so they could talk about her situation without embarrassing her. At night, they shared these words with their husbands, who also began using them.

Another common account is that young men from the Singley, Miller, Wallach, and McSpadden families were the original speakers and developers, creating the language as a way to talk about subjects that were not appropriate for children and women to hear. This was important as all members of the family worked together in the hop fields. From there, any gathering or activity that drew men together—visiting at the bar, sheep shearing, baseball, or hunting—was an opportunity for them to display their own adeptness at coining new words and hone their Boont skills. Over time, many women were also "harpin Boont."

World War I caused many young men from the core group to leave Anderson Valley. No new words were coined and the language began to fade away. Descendents of those early Boontners stepped in, keeping the dialect alive. In 1963, a feature release by the *Associated Press* created national interest in the invented language. Then in the early 1970s, Charles Adams, Professor of English at Chico State University, published *Boontling—An American Lingo*, which has had wide distribution. The Boontling Club and Historical Society continue to work to keep this wonderful language alive.

SAMPLE OF THE BOONT LANGUAGE: bahl (good), ot'n (working), Boont Region (Anderson Valley), Boont (Boonville or Boontling), Poleeko (Philo), Iteville (Navarro), High Roller Region (Yorkville), pikin (traveling), drearies (mountains), harpin (speaking), Bluejay Region (Philo area), and Boontners (those who speak Boontling).

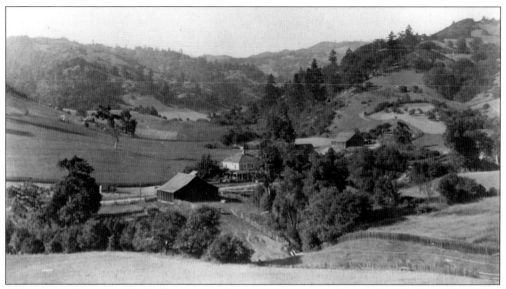

This is an overview of the Belk Region, about six miles east of Boonville. It shows the valley, which was home to a large hop field during the late 1800s and early 1900s. It was here that the strange language called Boontling originated.

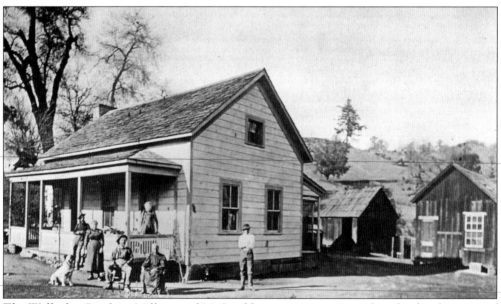

The Wallachs, Singleys, Millers, and McSpaddens were instrumental in the development of Boontling. This is the William Wallach duff nook (home). Remnants of this homestead are still standing in Bell Valley. The language they began testifies to their wit, intellect, and keen observations.

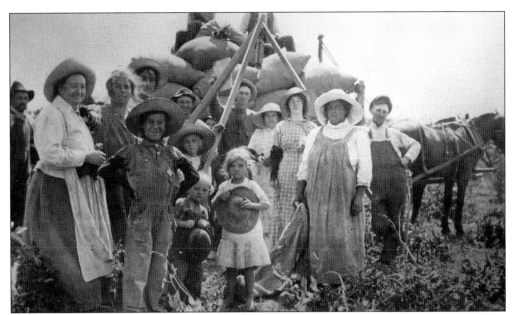

These families were ot'n hops in the Bluejay Region. At the end of the day, they bagged the hops. They were then loaded on wagons and taken to the hop kiln.

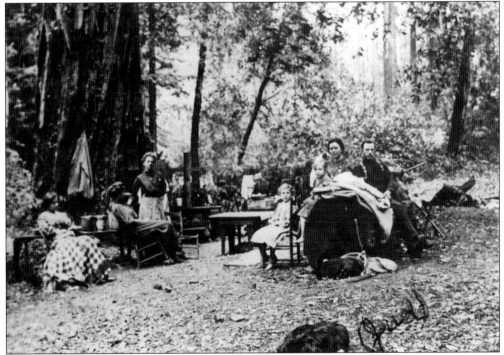

The hop fields brought welcome work to many families in the area who set up hop camps while in the fields, as shown in this 1908 photograph. Pictured, from left to right, are the dog Jud, Vera Rawles-Babcock, Blanche Brown, unidentified, Kelva Prather, Dorothy Chipman, Madge Brown (Hendley), and Bob Stump.

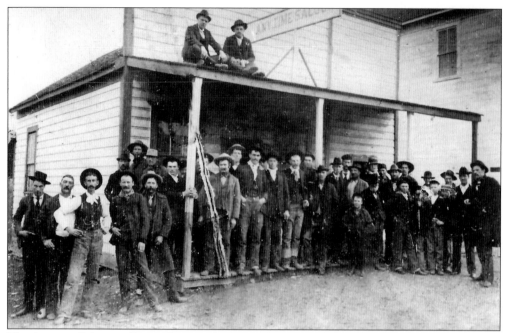

The Anytime Saloon in Boonville was a favorite gathering place, both as a hornin' region (saloon) and for harpin' Boont. D. P. Port Lawson, Jim Watson (owner), Emitt McGimpsey, Bill Rector, and George V. Vestal are the five men standing on the left. The boy is Sid Duff, the man in front on the far right is Pat Robinson, and Charlie Lawson was sitting on the roof next to the sign.

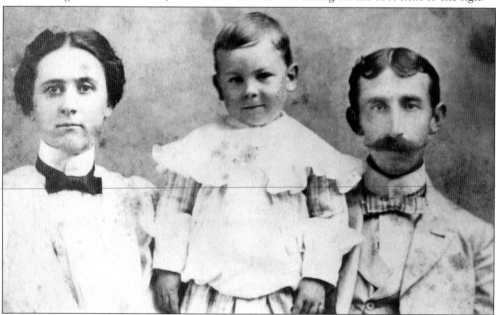

The women were fed up because their men spent too much time hornin (drinking), so they created a dry region. Emitt and Addie McGimsey owned the Anytime Saloon when it was jacked up and moved outside the dry region in 1903. It was renamed the Anyhow Saloon, so Boontners could get a horn "anyhow." Later, the Anyhow was moved back to Boont and used as a restaurant. It was then moved again, this time to Poleeko, where it still serves the valley as a restaurant.

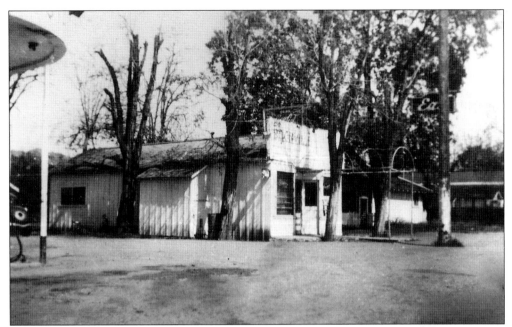

After the dry regions ended, a new hornin region, The Bucket of Blood, was built in downtown Boont. It is said many a Boontner spilled blood fighting their way out of this "hornin' region." Later, this building was torn down and replaced by the Boonville Lodge, which still serves as the local watering hole.

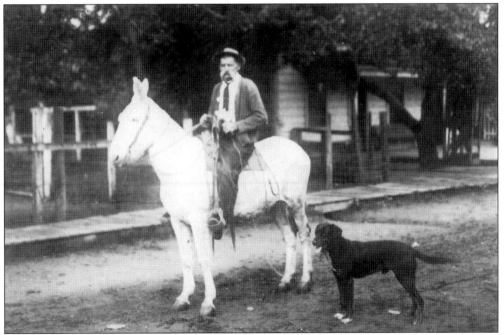

Boontling words were often coined from the names of people. Jeff Vestal, shown here on his white mule, owned the Missouri Hotel. He loved a good fire and it is said that no matter the time of year, there was always one in the fireplace of his hotel. He was also known for setting a fire to clear his lands outside of town. Soon "Jeffer" became the Boontling word for fire.

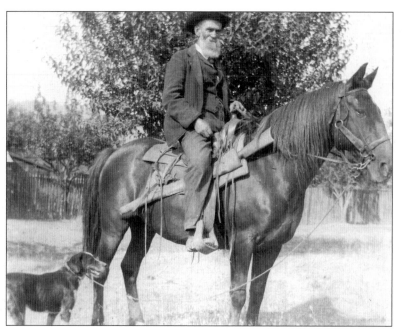

Z. C. (Zeese) Blivans, shown here with his horse Thurmann, loved his coffee. He probably drank more of it than anyone else in the valley. On hunting trips, Zeese brewed the coffee, which most said would float an egg. Hence, "zeese" became the Boontling word for coffee.

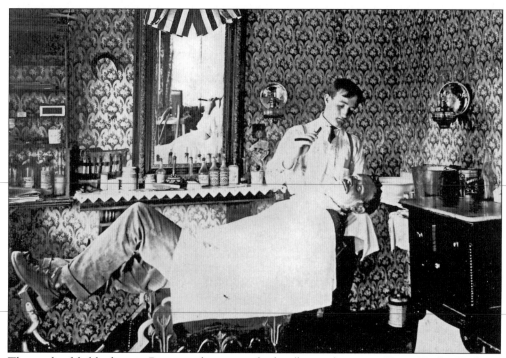

Those who felt like harpin Boont and getting a hedge (haircut) went to Harry Fitch's Hedgery (barbershop). On this day in 1906, Harry Fitch was giving a shave to Joe Rawles.

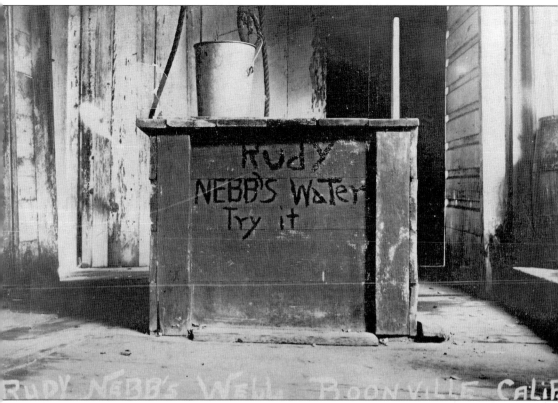

In the early 1900s, a mysterious traveler came to Boonville and stayed at the Anderson Valley Inn. This person was none other than famed cartoon writer Rudy Nebbs. When Nebbs took a taste of the ice-cold, crystal-clear water from the well at the inn, he immediately offered the hotel owners a tremendous sum for the well. Surprisingly, they refused. Nebbs stated, "I commend the public spirit of the people of Boonville in hanging on to this noble fountain. I cannot honor it more than bestowing my own name upon the well." It became a local joke and the Boontling name for good, clear water, "Rudy Nebbs," was coined. The well is shown in this picture around 1925 and is still in use today at the Missouri House.

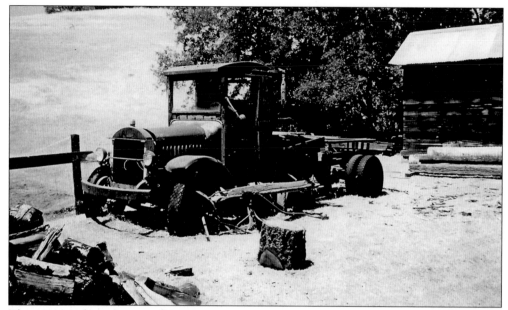

This 1929 Mack truck was used between 1939 and 1954 at the L. W. Lowrey sawmill in Yorkville. It hauled logs to the mill and delivered lumber throughout the valley. After its useful life, it sat in a corral on the Lowrey Ranch. In July 1987, the old truck was offered to "The Kimmeys of the Kodgy Moshes," which when translated from Boontling means "friends of the Old Machines," a local group of antique machine restorers.

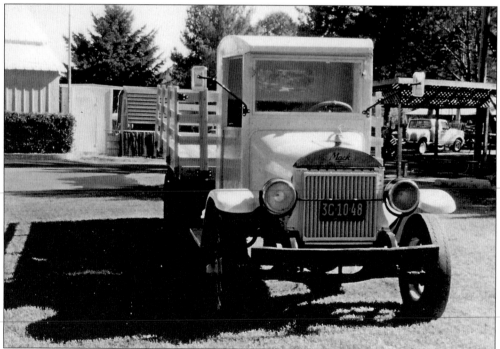

After six long years, the old Mack truck turned out to be a right "bahl moshe" (good auto machine). Many man-hours of toil went into the task, with great rewards, and it provided the kodgy kimmies (old men) a chance to harp a health of Boont (talk a heap of Boontling).

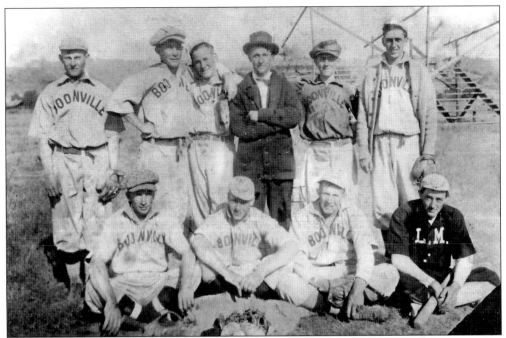

Buzz (baseball) was a favorite pastime in the valley and surrounding communities. The competition was intense, and high wagers were placed on the games. Many valley stories and Boontling words came from these games. It is said the word derived from the sound of the pitched ball and the click of the ball in the catcher's mitt. Pictured here are (sitting) Dutch Windom, unidentified, Monk Rawles, and unidentified; and (standing) Max Rawles, Ernest Rawles, unidentified, Fred Rawles, Phocian McGimpsey, and Jim Hutsel.

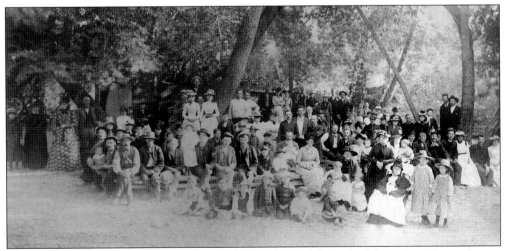

"Tidricks" (social gatherings) were often held in the beautiful woods of the valley. This gathering is a camp meeting. It took place at Con Creek, sometime before 1910. Churches sponsored the meetings, often bringing in evangelists. The Boontling word "Tidrick" is a combination of the words tea and drink. When folks got together they often drank tea, making it a social occasion, hence the origin of the word.

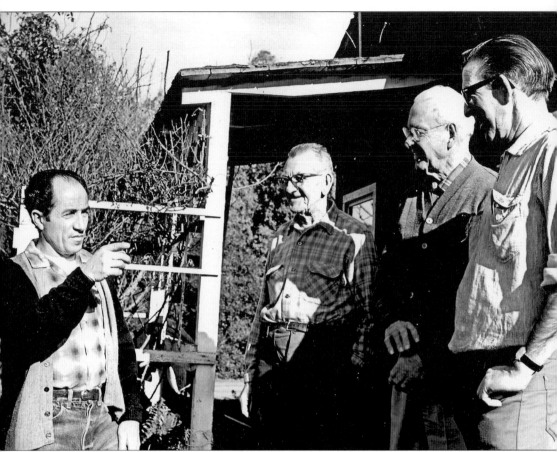

Boontners were known for their nicknames that derived from their occupations, appearance, habits, family ties, or sometimes an incident. At times these monikers also became Boontling words. Shown here are Boontners Robert "Chipmunk" Glover, Phocian "Mitchey" McGimpsey, Luster "Buzzard" Bivans and Jack "Wee Fuzz" June. "Chipmunk" is the Boontling word for hoard and Robert Glover was known as a hoarder. "Mitchey" was a shortened version of the last name McGimpsey. "Buzzard" Bivans lived in the high country above Boonville. He flew (like a buzzard) down to Boonville every day for school. "Wee Fuzz" was named after his dad Howard, who was the "fuzz" (justice of the peace). Many sons took on the nicknames of their fathers, adding the word wee for each generation. I'm sure this group was "harpin a healch of Boont" (talking a lot of Boontling).

Three

BAHL TIMES

In the early 1900s, many resorts throughout the valley offered horseback riding, hunting, and fishing, as well as effervescent healing water or river swimming and boating. Most were also known for excellent cuisine. Hotels were popular, with guests often spending the night dining, drinking, and dancing before settling in for a good night's sleep. Many ranches took "city boarders" for a few weeks in the summer.

The trip to Anderson Valley was arduous. Some guests traveled by train to Cloverdale or Ukiah, by stage to one of the stops in Anderson Valley (a nine-hour trip), then by wagon to the resort. Most people stayed at least a month. In addition to the depots in Cloverdale and Ukiah, trains ran between Wendling (Navarro) and Albion, and between the Signal Ridge area and Greenwood (Elk). Passengers traveled by boat from the city, then boarded trains to go inland. Later, as roads began to improve, city dwellers came by automobile.

Two families started resorts in the Philo area, a place known for its wonderful establishments. The Van Zandt family started Hazel Hill, Redwood View Resort, and Ray's Resort. Hazel Hill recently became a private residence, Redwood View Resort is still in the Van Zandt family, and Ray's Resort is now Wellspring Resort. Mary Ward and her brother James Hanen began the Pines, which recently became a private residence, and the Wards established the Highland Ranch, which is still offering great vacations in the country.

Wendling, now known as Navarro, boasted four hotels in an area called Dago Town, and a dance hall, movie hall, brothel, and jail in the northern section called Mill Town. Thus good times were had on both sides of town.

In 1927, Anderson Valley began hosting the Apple Show. Designed to draw attention to the wonderful apples of Anderson Valley, it also served as another way for outsiders to enjoy the area. When wineries became part of the Anderson Valley landscape, there was yet another reason for city dwellers to visit.

What outsiders could only enjoy on vacations, local residents enjoyed every day. Hunting, fishing, swimming, dining, and dancing have always provided the valley's young and old a good time.

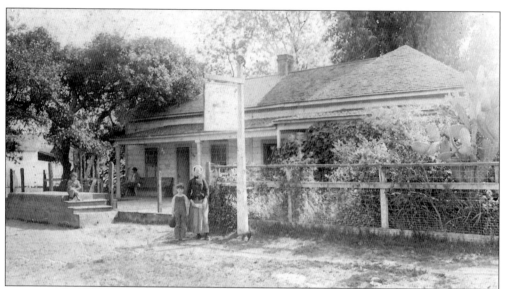

This Missouri Hotel, originally owned by Mr. Dillingham, was later sold to T. J. (Jeff) and Martha Vestal. In 1905, the name was changed to the Anderson Valley Hotel. Jeff Vestal would gather kerosene lamps from the rooms, place them on a large round table in the lobby, and fill them with kerosene. He then lit them all at once, believing that a hotel should be brightly lit. This building still stands next to the Boonville Post Office.

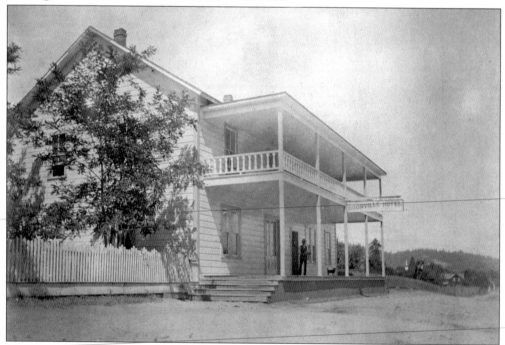

The Boonville Hotel, built in 1864 by Alonzo Kendall, is shown here in 1905. He named the area where it was constructed Kendall City. In the late 1920s, the hotel had to be moved back about 25 feet to accommodate the new highway. In those early valley days the hotel had many owners, including Stepp, Bostwick, Landerbee, Hayes, Peck, Christensen, Rickard, McGimsey, Duff, Sanders, Handley, and Berry. The Johnny Schmitt family runs the hotel today.

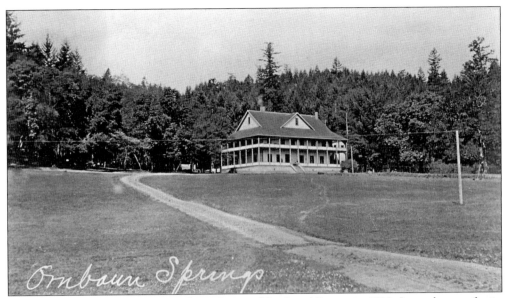

J. S. Ornbaun established the Ornbaun Springs Hotel and Resort in 1912. It was known for its spring of effervescent water, which many visitors claimed had healing powers. Locals joined the guests for dances on weekends. People came to the resort from the Bay Area, often staying for the entire summer. The Mailliard Family of San Francisco later purchased the property and it was never again a resort.

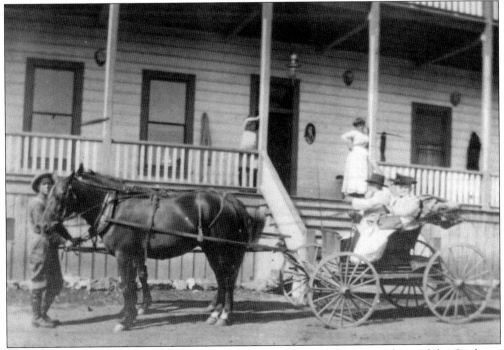

John Shipley (J. S.) Ornbaun and his wife Lucy Ann are in the buggy in front of the Ornbaun Springs Hotel and Resort. Horace Ornbaun's wife Meda is on the porch. J. S. hoped the success of the resort would bring him great wealth. While it was successful, it never made him rich.

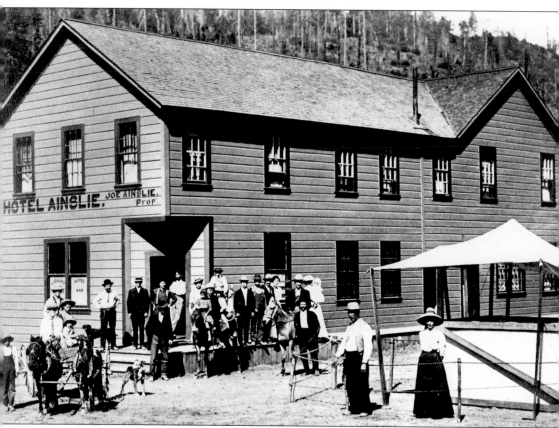

Poor roads made travel difficult and most valley residents worked six or seven days a week, so their entertainment came from local hotels, as shown by this gathering at the Hotel Ainslie. During one such gathering, a balloonist used large bellows to fill a balloon with hot air. The balloon had a bar across the bottom and the balloonist was wearing something that looked like a suitcase on his back. As the balloon filled, it began to rise against the ropes, holding it in place. Suddenly the man thrust the bellows aside, clutched the bar firmly in both hands, and shouted, "Let her go!" As the balloon floated gently upward, the man performed tricks on the bar that was on the bottom of the balloon before a tiny figure fell from it. The crowd gasped, but he was okay since he went on to work at Finney's store in Boonville.

The Van Zandt family began Hazel Hill in the late 1880s. Located on the Rancheria Creek in Philo, the resort began with four cabins in the redwoods. Mary Van Zandt was an excellent cook and it gained a good reputation. As it grew, more cabins were built and a social hall was added. It remained in the family until the 1920s. In 1944, the McDougalds bought the resort, renaming it Tumbling McD. It was a children's camp, adult dude ranch, and resort for many years.

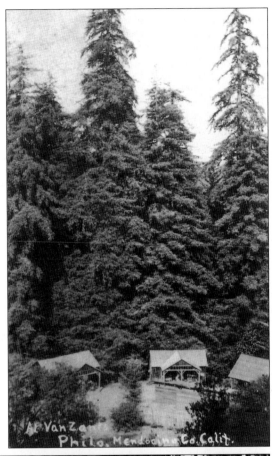

These guests of Hazel Hill, later called Van Zandt's, were boating on the Rancheria Creek around 1908. The river was a favorite spot for guests to boat and swim. Don Van Zandt and his wife, Alta, opened their own resort nearby on the Navarro River, naming it Redwood View Resort. Don's son Ben, his wife Alice and their children, today run this resort. Many of their guests are also multi-generational, carrying on the vacation traditions of their childhoods.

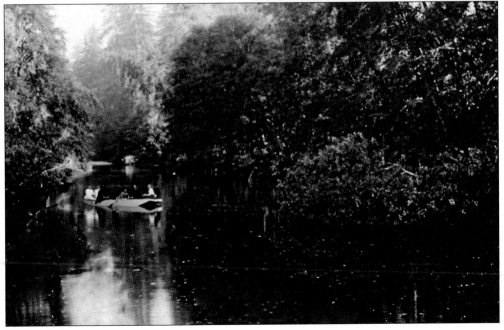

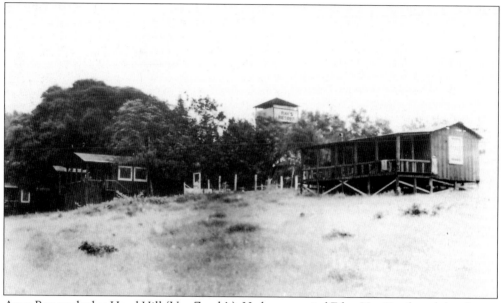

Avon Ray worked at Hazel Hill (Van Zandt's). He later married Edna Van Zandt and they began Ray's Resort, located downriver from Van Zandt's on the Navarro River. According to Avon's second wife, Lenore, the resort was started specifically to accommodate the overflow from Van Zandts. Upon Avon's death in the 1950s, Leonore continued to operate it until she sold it. In the 1970s, a new resort was born called Wellspring, which continues to operate today.

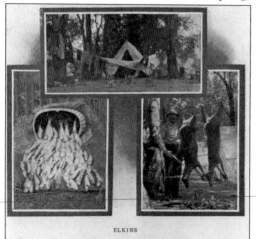

ELKINS

Elkins—Yorkville. Twenty-two miles from Cloverdale. By stage or private conveyance. Excellent trout fishing and hunting. In connection with resort is a good log cabin back in the mountains, about 5 miles, where guests can remain if they prefer. Will take parties out on hunting and camping trips. Also have fine place in the Redwoods for campers. Open April 1st to October 30th. Can accommodate 12. Rates, $1.00 to $2.00 per day; special rates on application. Address Mrs. R. L. Elkins, Yorkville, Mendocino County, Cal.

The Elkins Vacation Resort was located in the Yorkville area. Visitors could arrive by stage or private conveyance. As shown in their 1912 brochure, they offered hunting, camping trips, and excellent trout fishing. There were many of these small resorts in the valley, all advertising great hunting and fishing.

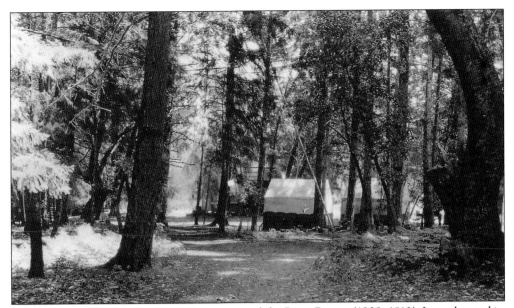

Mary Ward and her brother James Hanen started the Pines Resort (1908–1910). It was located in Philo where three streams join to form the Navarro River. The attractive cabins were spotlessly clean. The outdoor privies were discreetly set up in a line on the hillside below the cabins and shower rooms. The common room, adjacent to the large dining room, had a fireplace. Mary was a fabulous cook and often served 60 to 65 guests during the peak season.

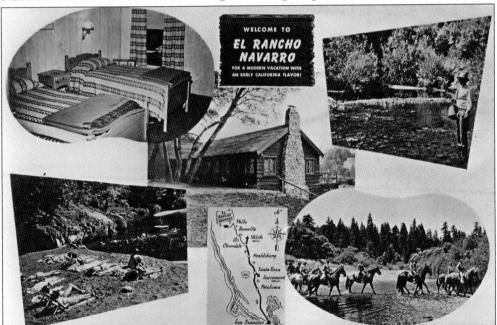

During the late 1940s and 1950s, the Pines Resort was owned and operated by Irving Newman as El Rancho Navarro. It was a children's camp and modern-day resort. It was later sold and became Shenoa. During the next several years, new resorts sprang up in the valley: the Shamrock Inn was located about two miles south of Boonville and the Bear Wallow Resort was located about four miles west of Boonville on Mountain View Road.

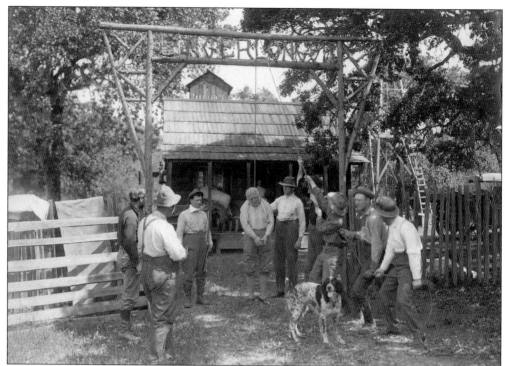

This group of friends was having fun at Doc Edwards's cabin. Doc may have been one of the first (but certainly not the last) city dwellers to have a second home in Anderson Valley. Their getaway, called Linger Longer, was on Indian Creek. Since the trip up from Oakland was long and arduous, they encouraged all to "linger longer." Doc, a dentist, later retired to his retreat.

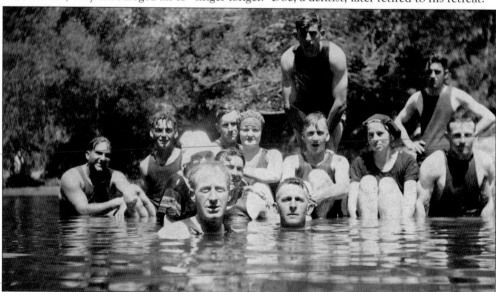

Where Anderson Creek made its big bend at Boonville was another favorite swimming hole. This group either included some very short people or they were just pretending to be in "up to their necks." Pictured, from left to right, are Ban Burger, Joe Cooney, Ronald Wallach, Vernon Rawles, Austin Rawles, Fred Rawles, Russie Rawles, and Max Rawles (ladies are unidentified).

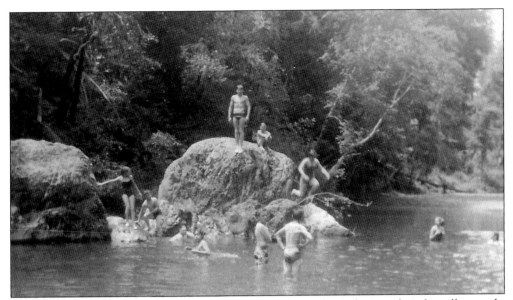

The swimming holes of Anderson Valley have always been the gathering place for valley youth. Pat Hulbert is swimming with friends during a 4-H camp at Five More Hole on the Navarro River in 1955.

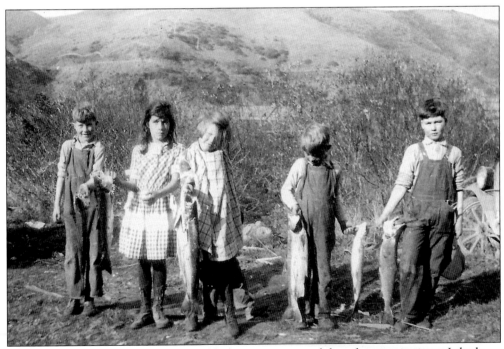

This photograph shows a gang of local kids enjoying one of their favorite pastimes. It looks as though they had very good luck and a whole passel of fun at the Price Ranch in 1923. Pictured here, from left to right, are Richard Day, Beth Day (Tolman), Irma Ruby Price (Hulbert), William (Bill) Day, and Jesse Beeson Price.

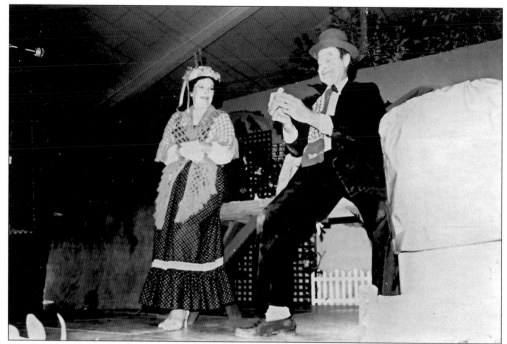

The community of Anderson Valley loves a good time. Like many communities, the amount of talent residing in the area is amazing. The Boont Town Players entertained themselves and the rest of the valley for many years with song, dance, and skits. Emil Rossi and Eva Holcomb, two members of the Boont Town Players, are pictured here in a skit. Today the Grange holds an annual community variety show and the valley's talented continue to entertain.

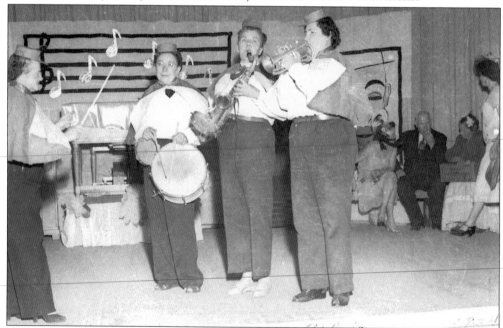

Bands have always been a big part of valley fun. These performers were performing at the Apple Hall in 1954. Pictured, from left to right, are Leone Goodhue, Ruby Fleck, Arlie Clark, and Arline McAbee.

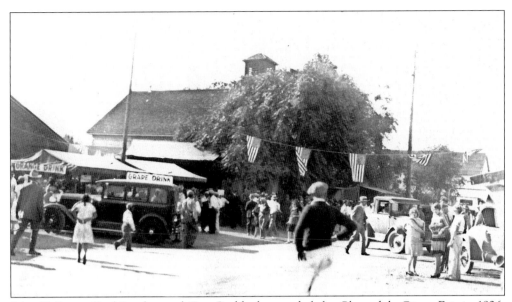

John T. Farrer, Fred Rawles, and Tom Ruddock attended the Cloverdale Citrus Fair in 1926. On the way home, they discussed having a similar fair in Anderson Valley. They called other townspeople together to discuss the idea and it was well received. The first Apple Show was put together in October 1927 and was an instant success. Judge Harwood June was the first director and Donald MacKintosh was the first fair manager.

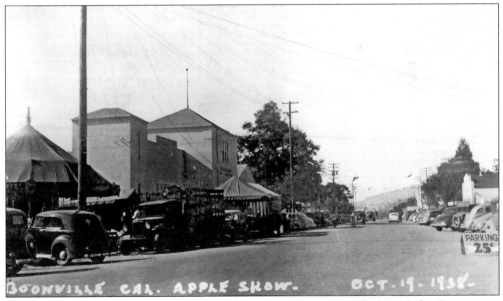

By 1937, Harwood June, Fred Rawles, Tom Ruddock, and Chester Estell had traveled to Sacramento, talked with legislators, and gained permission to list the fair as the "Mendocino County Fair and Apple Show." Pictured here on October 19, 1938, is the first pavilion. The community rallied together, building it with donated money, lumber, hardware, and labor.

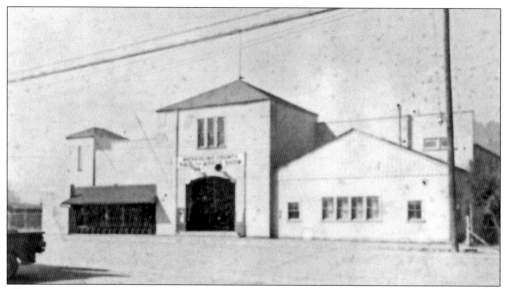

The original fair was constructed on an acre and a half of land. Today there are five exhibit buildings, four stock barns, and a rodeo arena on 35 acres. Boonville swells to capacity at fair time. Harwood June served as fair manager from 1937 to 1956 and when a new complex was built in 1958, the floriculture room was appropriately named "June Hall." Other long-time fair managers were Dick Winkler (14 years) and Jim Clow (17 years).

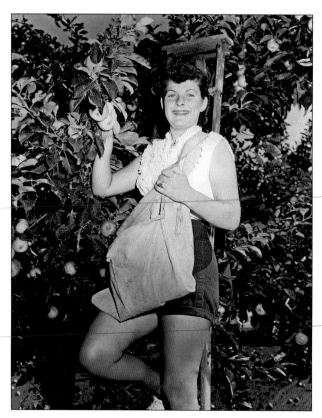

Miss Eva Pardini is shown here harvesting fine Anderson Valley apples that were displayed at the Apple Show on September 26, 27, and 28 in 1952. That year the fair also featured a rodeo, flower show, stock exhibits, dancing, a vaudeville show, and a carnival.

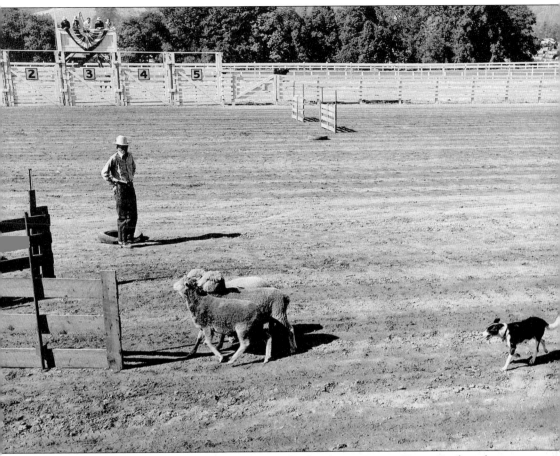

The Sheep Dog Trials, which began in 1976, are another big fair attraction. Ernest Pardini, shown here during one of the early trial years, works his prize sheep dog. In these contests, the dog has to put three sheep through the gates and into a corral on a timed basis. The most difficult part of the trial is working with only three sheep. It is much easier for a dog to perform with a large flock.

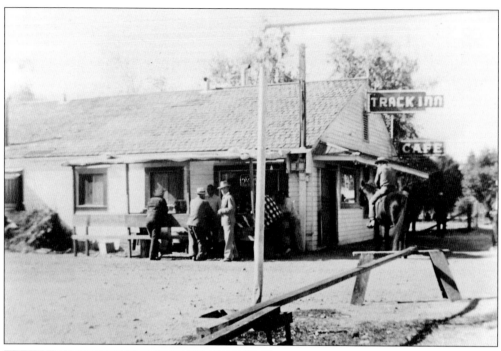

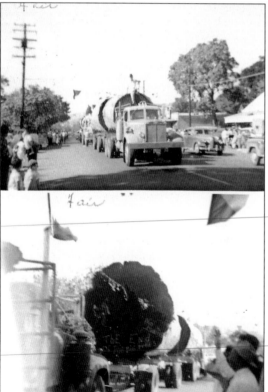

The Track Inn did not have enough room inside to accommodate the large fair crowds, so a beer bar was set up outside. It was often a rowdy time during the fair and rumor has it that on Saturday evening of the 1949 edition there were 14 fights going on at one time in three different bars. There is further hearsay that some of the strapping locals spent most of the evening going from bar to bar looking for a fight.

On Sunday, the fair features a parade. In the boom years, logging trucks often entered the parade under the guise of showing off their logs. Then, as it is now, it was against the law to haul wide, high, and overweight loads on the highway. Thus the loggers entered such loads in the parade and after it was over they drove on down the road, delivering the load to the Charles Lumber Mill. Harold Perry is standing next to logs measuring 8 to 12 feet in diameter.

Four

OT'N IN THE WOODS

The early settlers needed homes and the land was full of trees, so by the middle 1800s logging in Anderson Valley was underway. Most of the logging and milling took place in the northwestern part of the valley, making Hop Flat and Wendling booming mill towns. Railroads were built from Wendling to Albion and Signal Ridge to Greenwood (Elk). In addition to the railroads, ox and bull teams, horses and wagons, steam donkeys, and log-hauling cars carried the logs and lumber. Sawed lumber, railroad ties, shingles, grape stakes, hop poles, and fence posts were in great demand. Mills were built by John Gschwend, John Ornbaun, the Clow Brothers, Thomas Hiatt, Henry Irish, August Wehrspon, G. X. Wendling, and M. C. Triplett. Only the mill at Wendling sent lumber out of the area.

Tanbark harvesting was a major industry before 1900. Lands were being cleared of tan oaks, making room for homesteads and pasture. What a miracle it was that tan oak bark had a strong yellow, tannic acid used for tanning leather. The bark was hauled by train to Cloverdale then shipped to processing plants in the Bay Area. By 1940, the tanbark era was over.

The Depression and World War I ended this expansion period. In 1937, the railroad and parts from the Albion Lumber Company (previously Navarro Lumber Company) were torn out and shipped to Japan for scrap iron.

World War II brought the second boom period. Pre-war building in defense-related industries, such as shipbuilding, created a huge demand for lumber. Following the war, local economies grew, continuing the demand for wood products. Mill and logging operations sprang up like mushrooms in the fall. Trucks, caterpillars, cranes, and other machinery brought new efficiency.

The valley's population grew and schools were bursting at the seams. On Saturday night, the bars were packed. Downtown Boonville boasted three grocery stores, a ford dealership, several hardware stores and gas stations, a towing company, hotels, restaurants, J. T. Farrer's Merchandise Store, and the Boonville Lodge; it was a boom that lasted until the 1960s. Gone was the sound of logs splashing in the millpond, the smell of mill burners, the sight of huge log decks, and the clang of the green chain.

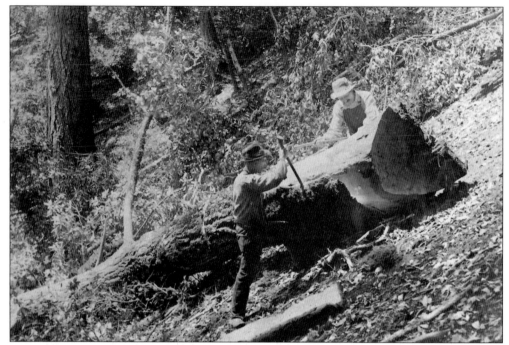

In the early 1900s, selling tanbark was a major industry and tan oak trees were plentiful in the area. They were not large trees and were often cleared from the land to create pasture. Tan oaks have a strong yellow, tannic acid in the bark used for tanning leather. The bark was peeled from trees and cut in four-foot lengths to be dried, and the trees were left to decay on the ground.

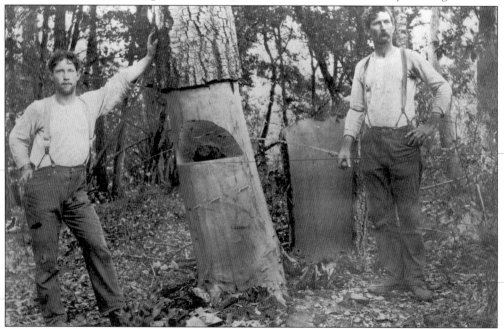

Tan Oak trees were peeled as shown here. Some trees were very small, so the bark was taken from while it was standing; this process was called Jay Hawking (in Boontling) and the people who harvested tanbark that way were called Jay Hawkers.

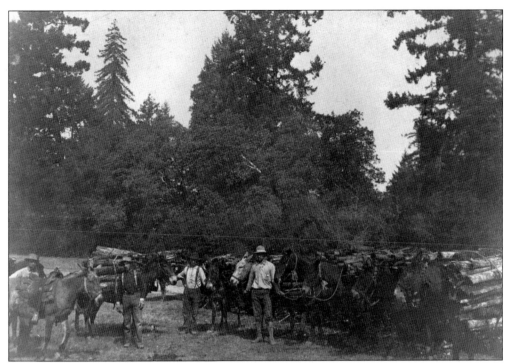

These mules are loaded with tanbark in 1910. The pack trains hauled the bark out of the back county before being loaded on wagons and usually shipped to processing plants in the Bay Area. In the 1900s, John Ward built a processing plant on Rancheria Creek near Yorkville.

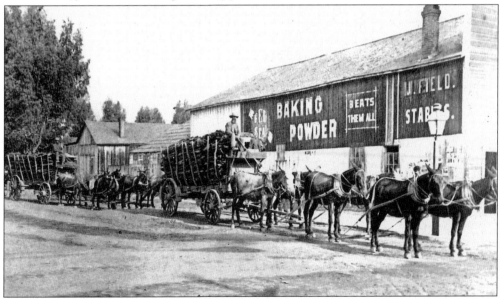

Two wagons loaded with tanbark are lined up waiting to be weighed. Irvin Ingram drove the back wagon and his father, Daniel "Cass" Ingram, drove the lead wagon. This photograph was taken at the railhead at Cloverdale where bark was loaded onto a train for delivery to a mill. In later tanbark years, trucks took over the hauling until this quick cash crop ended in the 1940s when the plants closed.

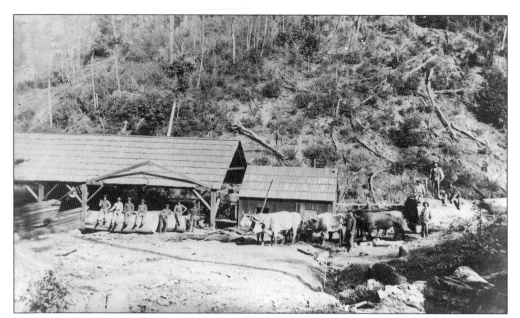

The Clow Mill, built in 1876 by George and Henry Clow, was located about four miles north of Boonville. Teams of oxen were used to skid the logs from the forest to the mill.

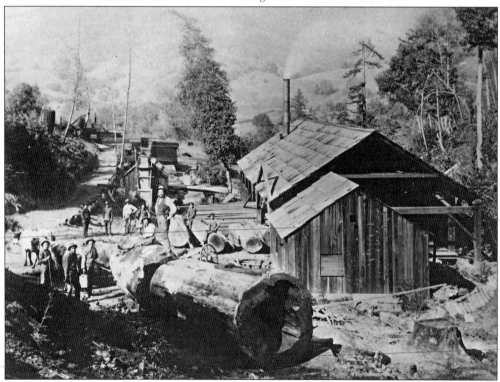

The Clow Mill ran for about 20 years, using the timber from 250 acres of land. The capacity of the mill was about 12,000 board feet of lumber per day, and it ran from dawn to dusk. These logs were pulled to the mill by oxen. Henry Clow is the Bull Puncher with the goad stick and is second from the left at the back in this photograph.

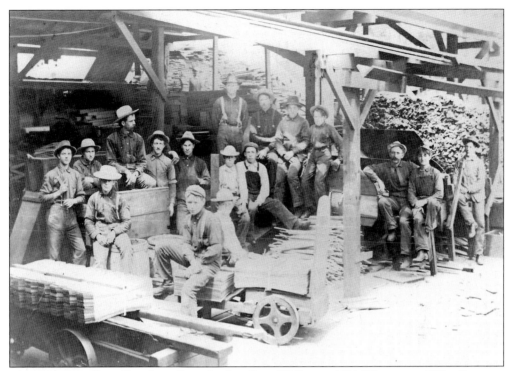

The G. X. Wendling Shingle Mill was built at Bear Wallow in 1901. The town of Wendling was named after his sawmill up the road near Mill Creek, but this was the first mill at the lower end of the valley.

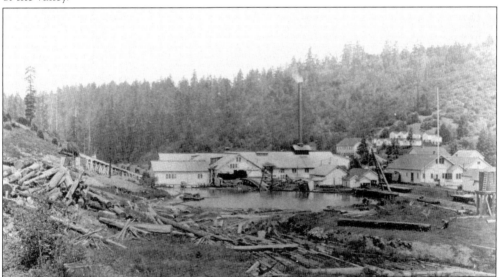

In 1905, Mr. Sterns purchased the Wendling Shingle Mill and it became a lumber mill. That same year the Albion to Wendling railroad was completed. Logs were unloaded into the millpond near the A-frame, and then floated from the arched tramway into the mill. Wood waste fired the mill's steam furnace. Water was obtained from springs via tunnels that were dug into the hillside, the longest of which was about 150 feet. These tunnels still provide water to some Navarro residents.

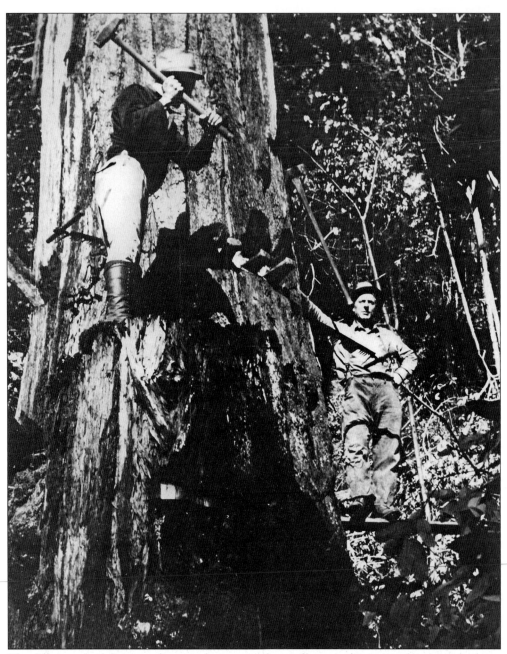

The faller on the left is standing on the stump of a smaller tree driving wedges into the large redwood tree. The tree being cut, like many in those days, was so tall that it would set back on the saw unless wedges were driven into the cut to force the direction of the fall. Because of the weight of the trees, it often took 10 to 15 wedges to get enough power to raise them. Today hydraulic jacks are used instead of wedges. The man on the right is standing on a springboard, which was placed on a notch chopped in the tree. The cutting was done with a crosscut saw and it took many hard man-hours to fall a tree. Once it was on the ground, it had to be bucked into lengths so the logger could handle it. Working in the woods was hard, dangerous work.

Charley Price and his son Alvy are chopping an undercut in a large redwood tree in late May 1926, working from a springboard. Their axes had 44-inch handles, so they could reach the center of the cut.

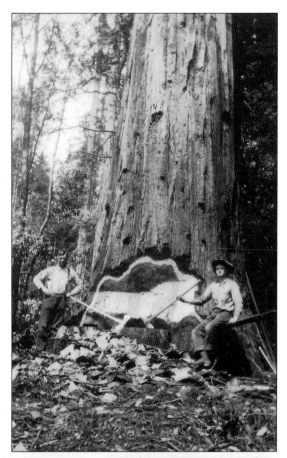

Alvy Price is laying on the butt of a tree that he and his father had just fallen in late 1926. The diameter of the tree measured just over 14 feet. Trees were still chopped and sawn by hand.

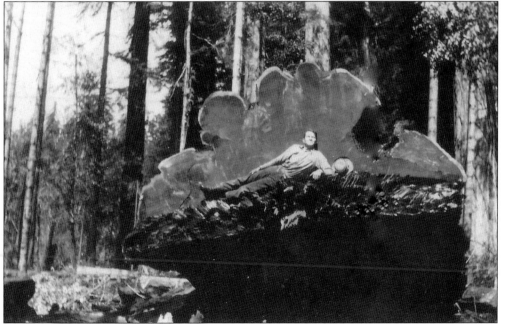

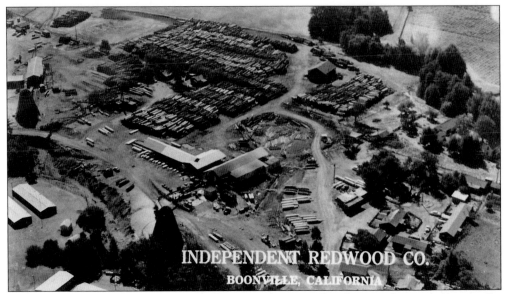

During the lumber boom of the late 1940s and 1950s, the valley floor was home to 40 sawmills. The hills of the valley housed another 10 to 12. The Independent Redwood Company, owned by Ellis and Harold Hess, was located behind the fairgrounds in Boonville. Most of the mills included mill housing for their employees. The splash of millponds, the smell of mill burners, the sight of log decks, and the clang of the green chain are some of the memories created in those times.

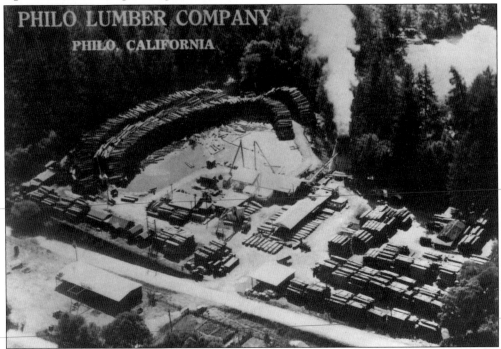

Pictured here is one of the longest lasting mills in the area, the Philo Lumber Company. It was established in 1939 and is still in operation today. Directly across from the Philo Mill is the I. and E. Lath Mill, which was started in 1956 and continues to run under the same ownership. In the photograph, the road running beside the mill is Highway 128.

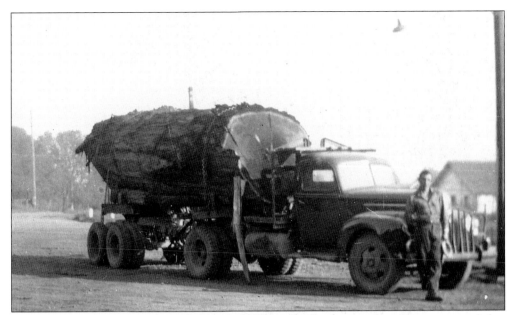

In the 1940s and 1950s, tough trucks like Ford, Chevrolet, International, and Reo were needed to haul logs from the forest. They were built to withstand the tremendous loads. This vehicle was one of several log and lumber trucks owned by Bert Rawley. The driver in front of the truck is Harold Perry, who, like many others of those times, came to the valley from Oklahoma seeking a job.

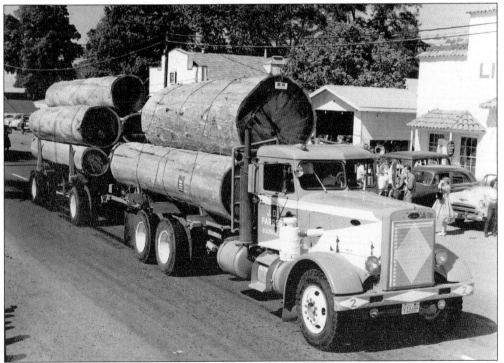

J. D. Farrer owned several logging trucks. His son Mike is driving this one in the 1959 fair parade. The logs hauled during this time were short, from 14 to 24 feet long, as loggers didn't have the ability to handle anything longer.

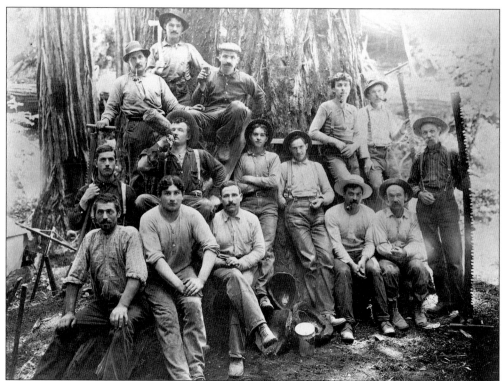

Crews that worked in the forest had to be strong young men. Pellegrino Tovani, second from the left, was just 17 years old when this picture was taken in 1900. Other members of the crew were Sam Blevins (with the pipe) and Charlie Mack (far right). The crew included fallers, buckers, and peelers.

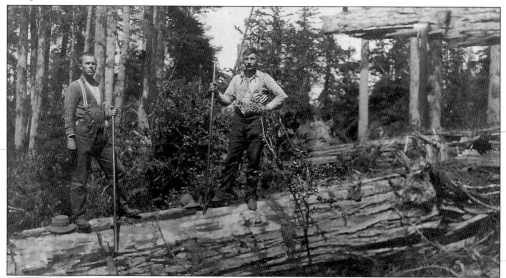

In the 1940s, redwood bark was not a usable product, so it was peeled from the logs and left in the forest. Oliver Moore could peel from 90,000 to 130,000 board feet per day. In the early years of the boom, peelers were paid 75¢ per 1,000 board feet; later, the wage was doubled. The logs had to be bark-free before the mill would accept them.

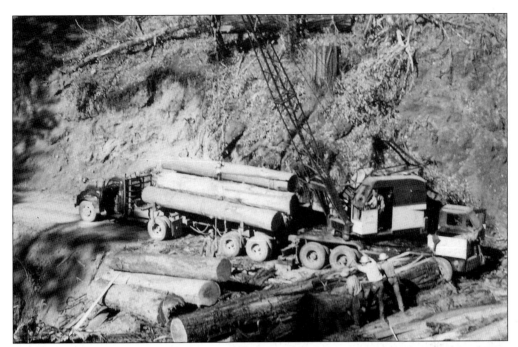

Gone were the ox and bull teams, horses and wagons, steam donkeys, railroad engines, and log-hauling cars. Crews were smaller and the industry was changing. This Link Belt Crane is loading logs onto a logging truck. When cranes were added to the logging process, landing areas could be much smaller. Jimmy Hughs is standing by the back wheel of the truck, Andrea Garatini was one of the peelers, Fred Jones was the crane operator, and Harry Avila owned the logging company.

When winter arrived, logging operations stopped. The equipment was moved to the mill yard, where it was checked and repaired. Word of job opportunities spread quickly and many people migrated to the valley. Mill camp houses were often built in three to four days, and locals often wondered if anyone was left in Arkansas and Oklahoma. While many of them were built with more focus on speed than quality, they provided good, warm housing for many families.

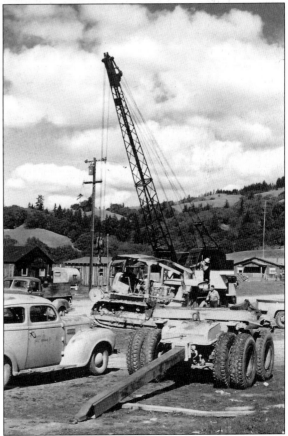

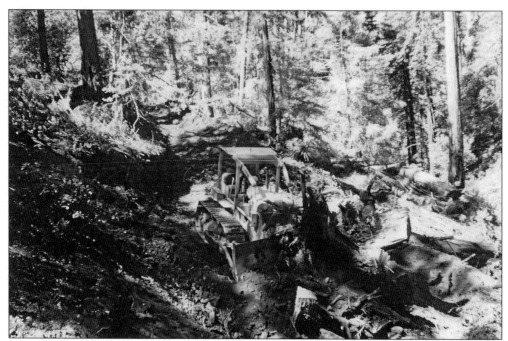

Not only did logging operations become more efficient, they could go places they couldn't reach in the early years. Later-model trucks could traverse steeper terrain and Caterpillar tractors, like this D-7, went in ahead of the crews, cutting in skid trails.

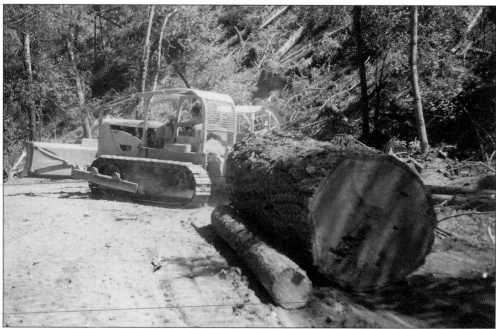

These two bulldozers (D-7 Caterpillar tractors) are pulling logs down the skid trail to the log landing. Bill Rawley is the operator. He worked for Martin and Quick Logging in the deep canyons and gulches of Ornbaun Valley.

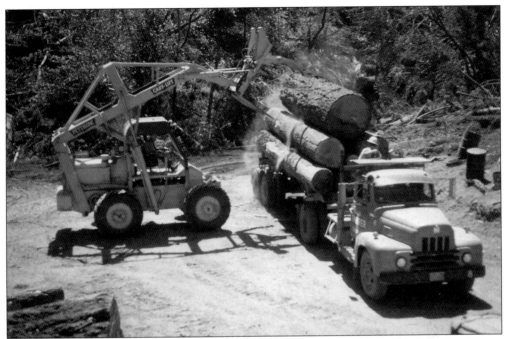

From the log landing, a Pettibone stacked the logs on the truck. The larger logs were put on top to balance the load.

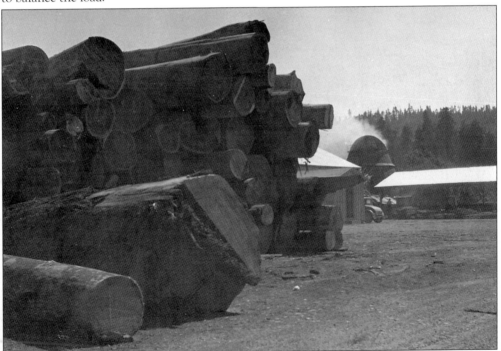

This log deck was located at the Ralph Burns Mill in the mid-1950s. Note the tee-pee burner in the background. A conveyor took sawdust and waste wood to be set ablaze before the burners were eventually outlawed. New uses for the "waste" were found, such as hauling it to press wood and/or particleboard plants.

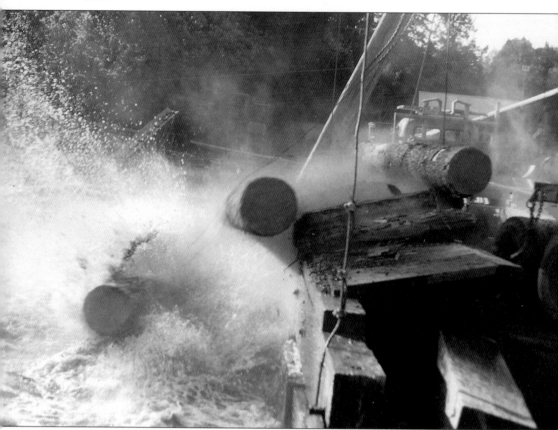

From the woods, the logging trucks headed to the mill, where they dumped their logs into the mill pond. Once there, the logs were either floated to the mill or directed to the back of the pond. Those that were floated to the back of the pond were lifted by crane and put on a cold deck to be held until needed by the mill, which was often in the winter when no new loads were coming to the mill.

Five

PIKIN IN THE DREARIES

Travel was so difficult in settlement days that the economy had to be largely self-sufficient. In the 1870s, a settler wrote that the valley was self-reliant except for the groceries that four-horse teams brought back twice a year from Cloverdale (a three-day trip). Once a year, drovers herded cattle, sheep, hogs, and turkeys on the long walk to market in Petaluma. Wool was pressed into bales and taken out on horseback. As production increased, more settlers came, all calling for better roads.

Early in the history of the valley, John Gschwend opened a road from Flynn Creek up the hill to the Navarro Ridge where it joined the road to Mendocino. Fruit from the valley traveled this route to the coastal market. John Gschwend also built the other valley "connector" route. In need of a market for his lumber, he pushed a bill through the California legislature authorizing the Mendocino County supervisors to grant a permit to construct a toll road over what was known at the time as the Anderson Valley Trail. The trail crossed the mountain from Boonville to an intersection that seemed a long way (two miles) south of Ukiah. The road cost $10,000 to build. In an attempt to recuperate some of the expense, Gschwend operated it as a toll road until shortly before the turn of the century when it was incorporated into the county road system.

Eventually, the county took over the wagon trails and made improvements, but with travel increasing and limited funds for maintenance, the roads were often in poor condition, especially in the winter. Locals knew hazardous areas by name and they became valley landmarks: Dobe Lane, Fairbanks Grade, and Clow Hill are just a few.

On April 24, 1923, the state began building a magnificent highway from the McDonald Ranch to the Pacific Ocean named McDonald to the Sea. Later, this became Highway 128. Today both are well-maintained state roads. However, they still contain many curves, discouraging those with faint hearts and stomachs.

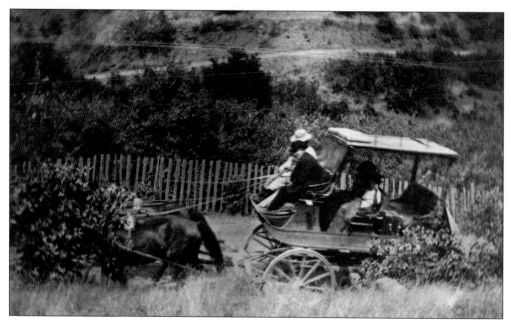

In the days prior to the 1900s, traveling in and out of Anderson Valley was a painstaking task. With the best of conditions, it was a long day's trip one way from the valley to Cloverdale, and another to return. In the winter months, during a storm it was often impossible to negotiate the rutted and muddy roads and swollen streams. The Cloverdale to Boonville Stage is shown here as it makes its way along the valley.

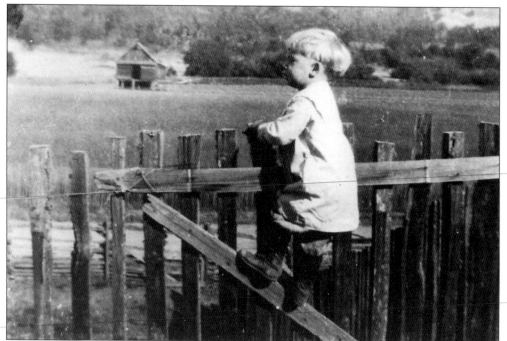

Most of the harnesses on the teams of horses had little bells on them in order for wagon drivers to hear an oncoming wagon. Here, little Everett "Buck" Ingram has heard the team bells coming and is waiting for them to pass so he can wave to the driver.

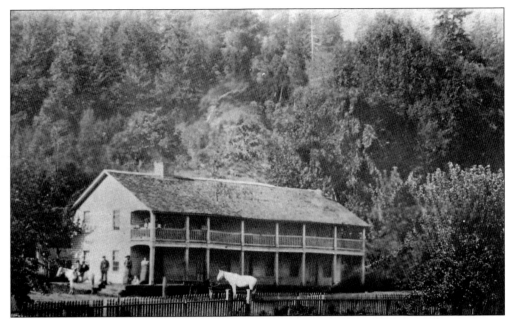

The Mountain House, shown here in 1875, was located on the McDonald Ranch. It was a famous stage stop where passengers could rest and have something to eat before continuing on to Hopland and Ukiah. While the passengers were getting refreshed, the drivers changed to fresh horses. Some people stayed overnight, waiting to catch a stage for the trip on to Boonville and the coast.

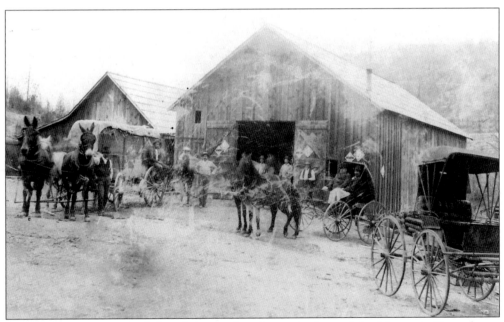

The freight wagon on the left and the two buggies are in front of the Mountain House barns where the road forked. The right fork went to Hopland and Ukiah, and the left went to Boonville and Wendling. The road to Anderson Valley and on to the coast acquired the name McDonald to the Sea Highway as it ran from the McDonald Ranch to the ocean. This photograph was taken in the 1880s.

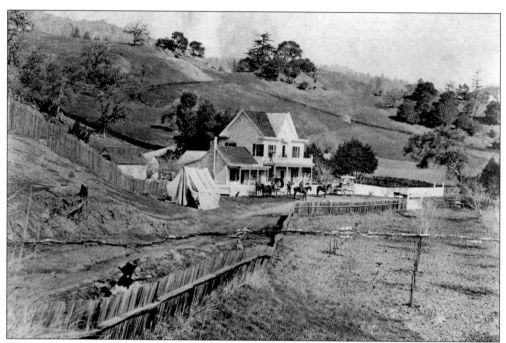

The Yorkville Hotel and stage stop was built in 1860; note the stage to the right of the hotel. The hotel was owned and operated by E. M. Hiatt and his wife Elizabeth.

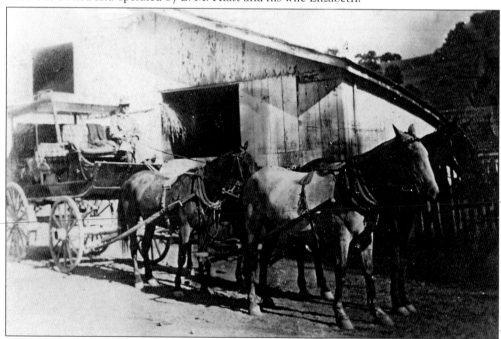

Mr. Ledford is driving this four-horse team that is pulling the Cloverdale to Boonville Stage as it stops in front of the Yorkville barn at the Yorkville Hotel. The stage made several stops between Cloverdale and Boonville. The first stop out of Cloverdale was the Mountain House, and then it went on to Hermitage, Whitehall, Yorkville, and Boonville. Each of these locations had extra horses to exchange for their tired steeds.

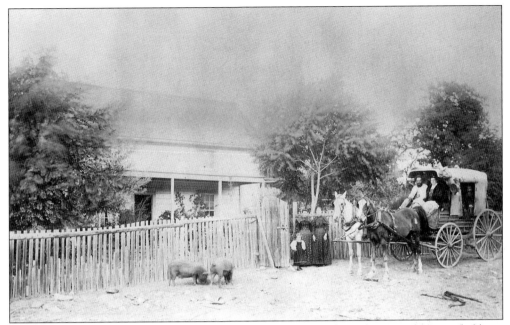

Here in front of the William J. Rose home, just north of Boonville, is the stage that is probably en route to Albion, *c.* 1900. Pictured are Sidney Rose, Martha Rose, Mary Jane Rose, and William James Rose (stage driver); others in the stage are unknown. This house is now the home of Albert Prather, a multi-generation valley sheep rancher.

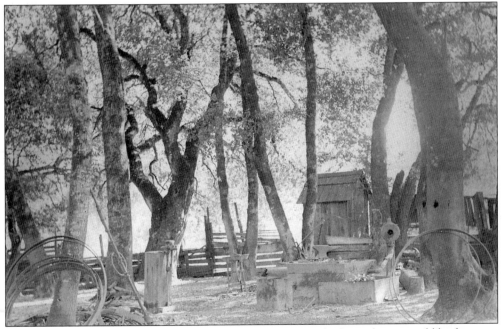

This is a view of the blacksmith area at Ed Guntly's Grove. The larger hoops could be for water or wine tanks, and the smaller ones could be wagon tires. Horseshoes, mule shoes, ranch tools, wagon wheels, or wine tank hoops—blacksmiths did it all.

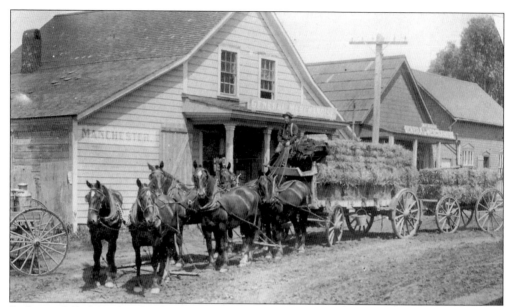

In front of the Manchester Store is a freight wagon and trailer loaded with hay. The six-horse team belonged to Bill Lawson and the driver is Jap Hitchcock. The wagons belonged to Walter Gschwend of Christine. The freight wagons operated much as freight trucks do today as they moved goods to any place, at any time.

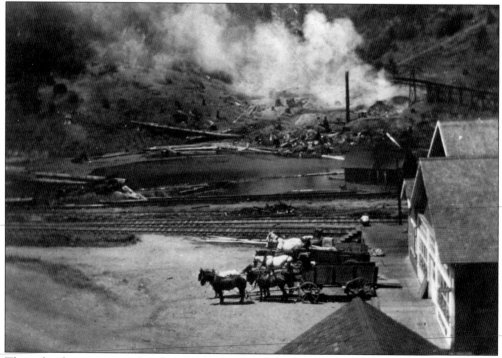

These freight wagons are lined up in front of the Wendling Store and were probably bringing goods from Cloverdale, Santa Rosa, or even Petaluma. The mill pond was across the tracks from the store. A conveyor carried sawdust waste from the mill, dumping it on the ground, where it was burned.

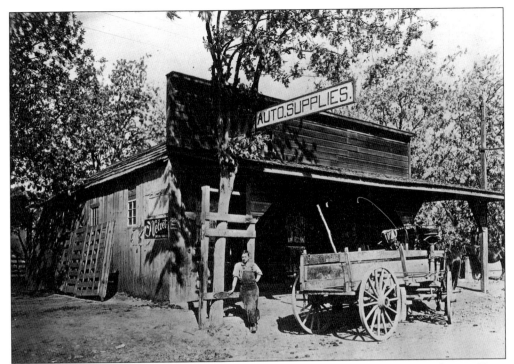

Dick Fitch is standing in front of his blacksmith shop in downtown Boonville in 1906. The sign "Auto Supplies" shows that automobiles were becoming another mode of travel in the valley. While there were only a few in the valley at the time, road conditions made repairs a common occurrence.

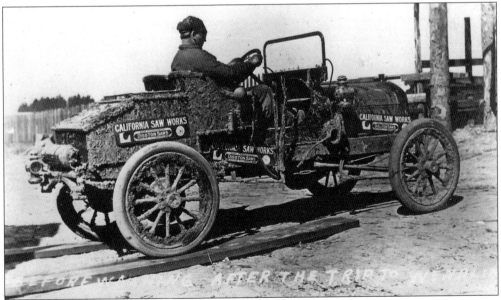

As can be seen in this 1914 photograph, the roads were far from desirable. This gentleman was a salesman for the California Saw Works on his way to Wendling to sell saws to the mill. While his car reflected the condition of the road, he made sure his advertising signs were free of mud. In this era, the roads received minimum maintenance.

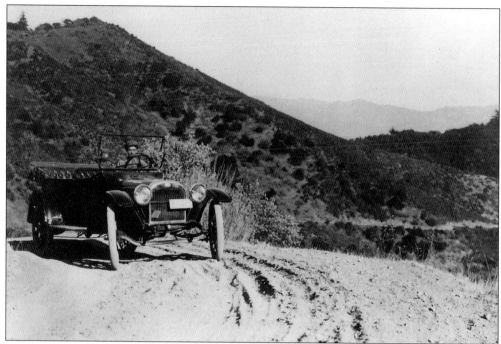

Frank Gowan is driving Johnny Switzer's 1916 Buick. The roadway was two wheel tracks wide and tires got lost in the dust. This road was called "Poor Way," as it was a poor route to Ukiah. Until the 1940s, many valley people went to Ukiah via the Mountain House to Hopland Road. The Ukiah Road was eventually taken over by the county, and in 1967 it became State Route 253.

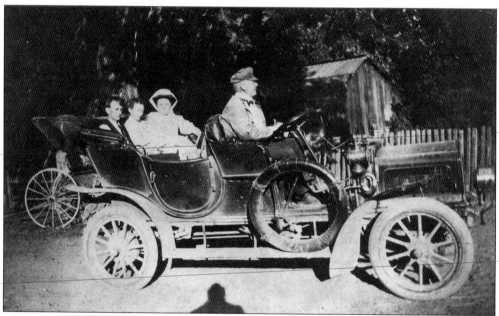

Automobiles (in front) were replacing buggies (in back). This was the first White Steamer to arrive in Anderson Valley and was most likely a "summer" car.

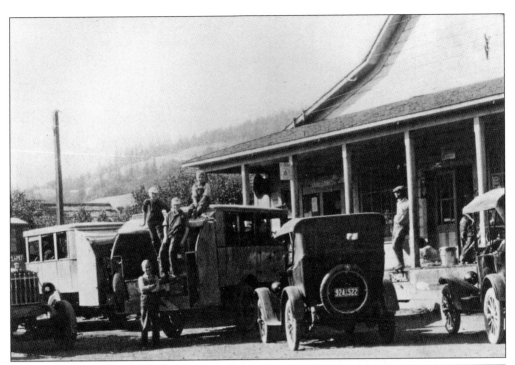

The two larger enclosed vehicles parked in front of George Johnson's Store and Post Office in Philo are passenger and mail stages, from around 1923. The stages met at Philo, coming from Cloverdale and Yorkville, as well as Wendling and Christine. Pictured at left are Irvin Herbert and his 1908 truck near the Mountain House on the old Yorkville to Hopland Road. It appears he is experiencing mechanical difficulty. Driving on the narrow, mostly one-lane roads was treacherous because the old trucks made so much noise that they could not hear the oncoming horses and wagons. Often the wagon driver would lose control of his horses, causing tempers to flare.

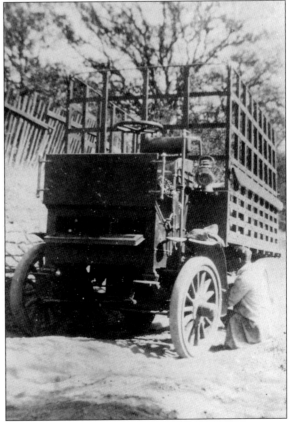

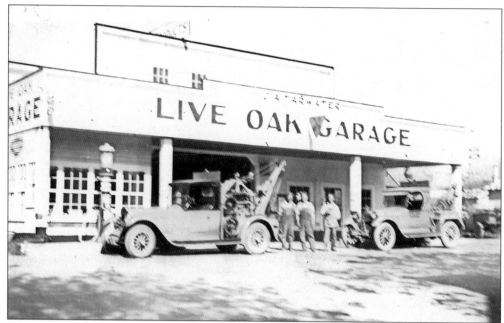

The Live Oak Garage in Boonville was owned and operated by C. A. Tarwater, known to the locals as "Cat." He was a skilled mechanic and he built the two tow cars pictured here. The one on the left is a 1932 Reo and the one on the right is a 1926 Packard sedan. The Live Oak building still stands in the center of Boonville.

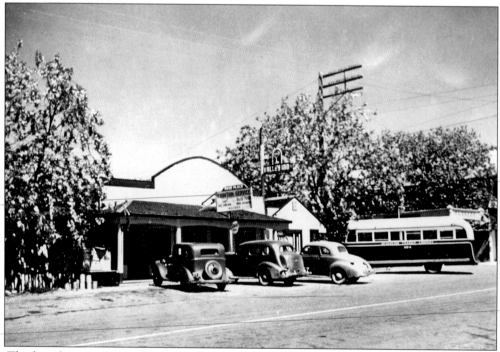

This bus, shown in front of Weise's Valley Inn in Boonville, was owned by the Mendocino Transit Company, which ran daily from Fort Bragg to Santa Rosa. In the mid- to late 1940s, this was the only public transportation in Anderson Valley.

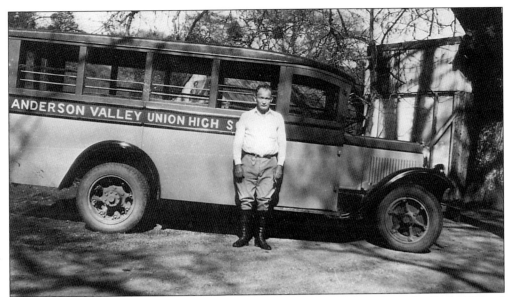

Ray Smoot is standing next to a 1928 Dodge school bus, which he drove from the Gaskill School south of Yorkville to the Anderson Valley High School. He drove buses in the area for 19 years that included school functions in Point Arena, Mendocino, and Fort Bragg. The seats in this bus ran lengthwise instead of crosswise. When the bus stopped suddenly, the pupils would all slide to the front of the bus.

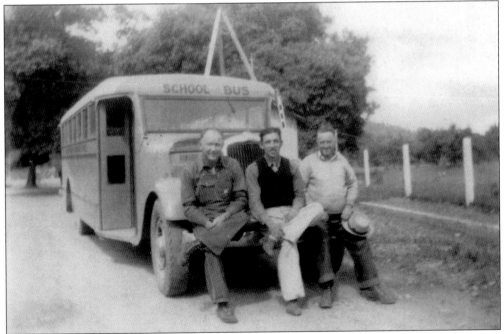

Pictured, from left to right, are Ray Smoot, Charley McCallister, and Dave Boyd, three bus drivers for Anderson Valley High School during the early 1940s. Dave drove this 60-passenger 1936 Dodge bus from Navarro to Boonville and also chauffeured for school functions in Hopland, Ukiah, Laytonville, and Lake County. Charley drove a converted Packard Hearse from Vinegar Hill and Signal Ridge to Boonville.

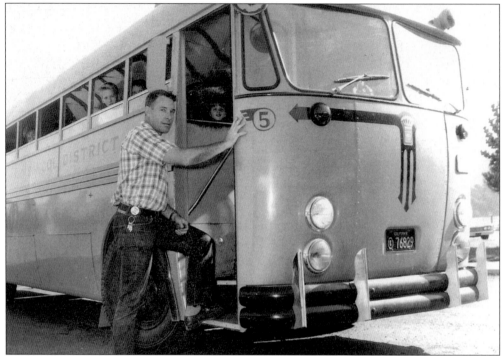

For 30 years, kids swore Ray Ingram had "eyes in the back of this head." Ray started driving the bus for the Anderson Valley schools in 1948–1949 and retired 30 years later. Ray's wife, Barbara, remembers that when Ray directed a student off the bus for the day, the child and parents often met the bus together on the day of his or her return to make sure proper apologies were made.

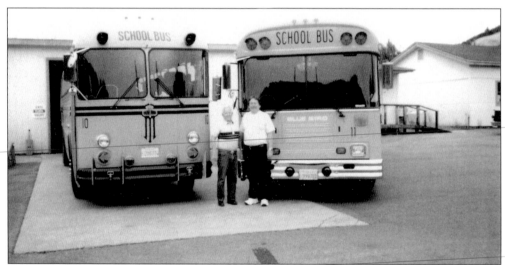

Shorty Adams has been driving valley school buses since 1958. He has received several honors, including a One Million Safe Mile Award, a Two Million Safe Mile Award, and the California Driver of the Year Award. As of today, he has driven 2,163,000 accident-free miles. Shorty's pleasant, but firm manner puts him in charge on his bus. His son Doug, who also drives school bus in the valley, has learned from the best.

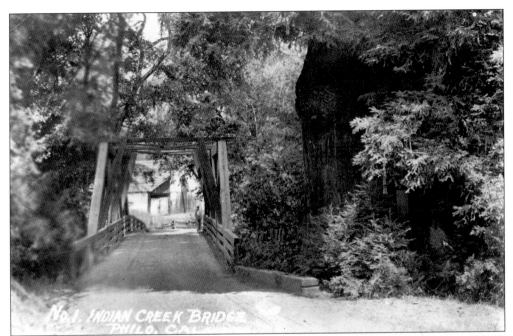

This photograph of the bridge, which spans Indian Creek just south of Philo, was taken around 1916. The barn on the other end of the bridge was the Ruddock barn. This was one of two bridges that were major links between Boonville and Philo. Rancheria Creek, Indian Creek, Anderson Creek, and the Navarro River all come together just a short distance downstream from the bridge.

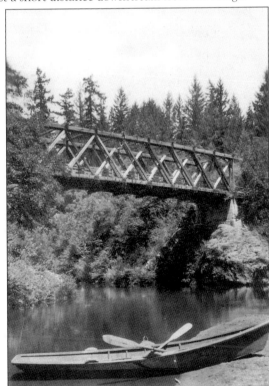

This bridge crosses the Navarro River on the road to Greenwood and supported many loads of lumber during the timber boom of the 1940s. It was replaced with a concrete bridge in the early 1950s. The swimming hole under the bridge was known as River Rest and was a favorite among residents.

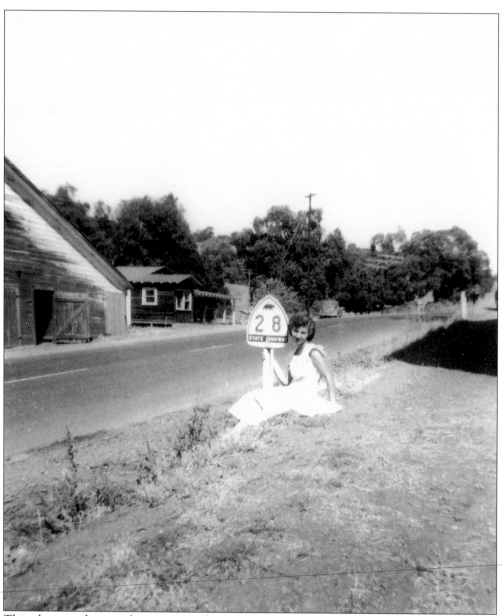

This photograph was taken in 1948 when the highway was still Route 28. Prior to 1933, the highway from Cloverdale to Mountain House, Hopland, and Ukiah was Route 1 and later Route 101 before becoming Route 28. In the late 1940s, Route 28 was changed to its present number, 128. George Washington and Mabel Hiatt lived in the house next to the barn with their two daughters, Missy and Marilyn.

Six

HIGH ROLLER REGION

In 1856, Cleveland Murray and his family settled where Calti Creek empties into Rancheria Creek, the site of an Indian rancheria. Later, John Wesley McAbee and his family arrived, settling on 700 acres across the creek form the Murrays. The Stubblefield party arrived in 1865 that included Robert, daughter Josephine and husband Patric Adams, and daughter Mary Ann and husband Richard York. They chose a home on 700 acres about one mile from the Murray Ranch, which was called the Stubblefield Place. Later, following Mr. Murray's death, his wife Susan married Mr. Stubblefield and they left the area, moving closer to the town of Boonville. Mr. York remained on the Stubblefield settlement.

The original inhabitants of the rancheria, the Ma-cu-maks, encountered white settlers before the Murray party's arrival and told them of an alarming visit when they witnessed "a thunder stick." It is believed those visitors were Russian explorers who settled at Fort Ross. Later, a few Spaniards settled in the area for a short time. The Ma-cu-maks grew to trust the Spaniards, and customs and language were shared. They were gone when the Murray party arrived, but due to those earlier amicable relations, the Ma-cu-maks and these new white settlers were able to live together peacefully.

In the little valley of old Yorkville, E. M. Hiatt arrived, purchasing lands near the York Ranch. Hiatt and Richard York were the "fathers" of Yorkville. Nearby, Rene Burger and his wife ,Elizabeth Gschwend, owned the large Burger Ranch. He was a well-known, old-time sheep man. The first store in old Yorkville was run by their son Hale and his new bride, Mildred. Their daughter Georgia married Wayne Lowry, who later started the first sawmill in the area at a spot known as the Oaks.

The current community of Yorkville was born in 1937, when Rancheria Creek flooded its banks and washed away the old Yorkville Post Office. It was moved three miles south to the Prather store, a settlement that until then had been called Whitehall (the name was changed to Yorkville). Further up the road were two other settlements, Hermitage and Mountain House, which began as stage stops.

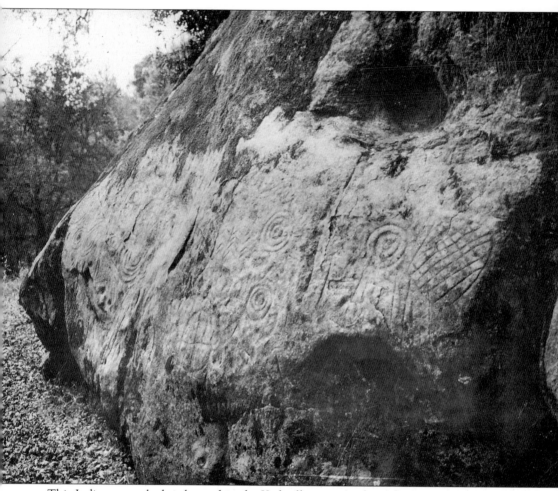

This Indian petroglyph is located in the Yorkville area. Anthropologists are not certain when the markings were made as they are not consistent with petroglyphs created by the Pomo. It is therefore possible that they are from a pre-Pomo era. The markings made by the Pomo were grooves, not circles as shown here. Pomo woman, who were having difficulty conceiving, created the grooves by using knives. They then took the dust from the cuts and decorated their bodies, and before leaving they would ask for a child. They viewed the rocks as holy places and believed that by making contact with them they would be granted fecundity.

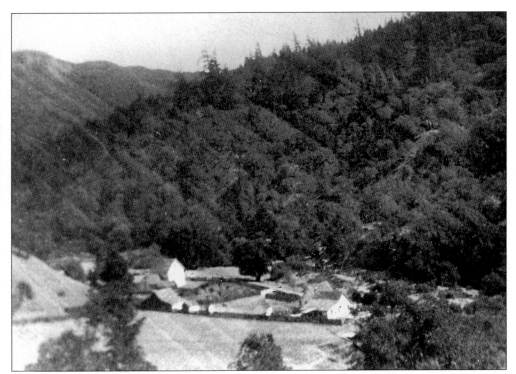

This overview of Yorkville was taken in 1907. At that time, the community center was across from Hibbard Road, about three miles north of the current town of Yorkville. The home shown on the right belonged to Charles Hiatt and the second Yorkville Post Office was next door. The tall building was the Burger Store. The barn and house are still in use today.

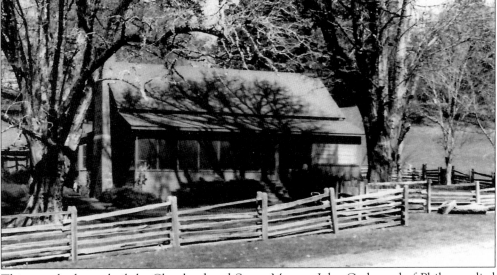

This was the home built by Cleveland and Susan Murray; John Gschwend of Philo supplied the lumber. Susan was the first "doctor" in the valley. One of her first white patients was Mrs. Anderson, the "mother of Anderson Valley." Word spread and soon everyone throughout the valley knew to send for Susan (Grandma Stubblefield) when they needed a doctor. Susan died in 1895, close to the time that Doc Brown, the second valley doctor, arrived.

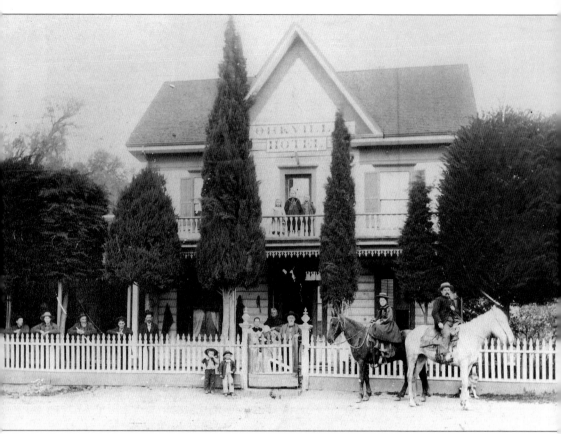

In 1867, E. M. Hiatt built this large two-story house, which he made into a hotel. He constructed large barns and outbuildings, which were used as a stage stop and blacksmith shop. At this time, the community had no name. Both E. M. Hiatt and Richard York wanted the town to be their namesake, so they decided to play a game of cards with the town taking the winner's name and the loser becoming the postmaster. York must have won, as the town was named Yorkville, and the first post office was located in the front of E. M. Hiatt's hotel. E. M. was postmaster until he retired in 1889.

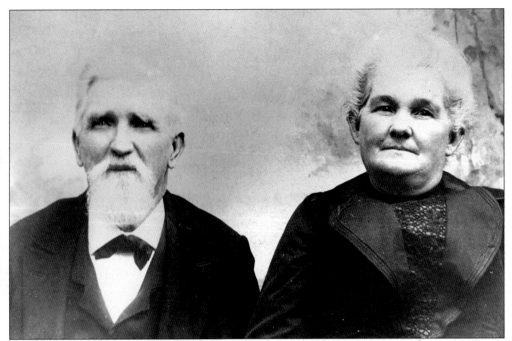

E. M. Hiatt purchased a ranch from York in 1867 and it became one of the finest sheep ranches in the valley. Elijah purchased additional land as it became available and by 1909, the year he died, he owned 6,000 acres. He and his wife Elizabeth raised a large family of four sons and six daughters. Their son Charles took over as postmaster when E. M. retired.

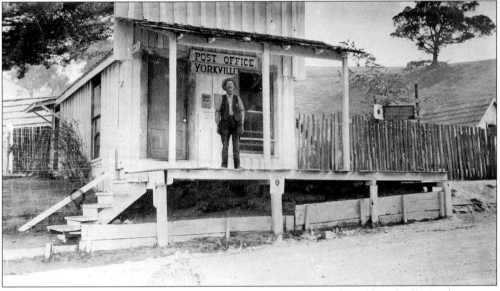

Charles Hiatt was the postmaster of the second post office, located in old Yorkville. In the winter of 1937, a flood washed it down Rancheria Creek. Allie Prather and later Emmabelle Witherell were postmasters at the new post office that opened in Allie's Store three miles to the south. Later, Leo Marcott became postmaster, moving the post office to his home. Local volunteers, on land donated by Austin and Sylvia Hulbert, built today's post office, and Joanne Aronsen is the postmaster.

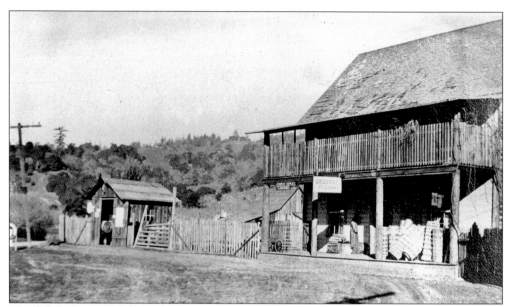

The Burger Store sold whatever was needed in the community. They stocked groceries, fencing, and hardware, as well as clothing and other items. If they did not have it in stock, they would order it. Delivery could take a few days or several weeks, depending on the item. The nearest railroad depot was in Cloverdale. Freight wagons would pick up the freight at the depot and deliver it to the store. The proprietors of the store were Mr. and Mrs. Hale Burger.

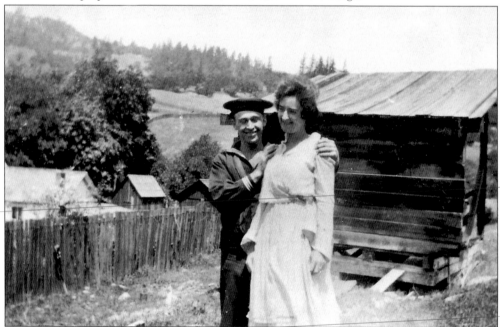

Hale and Mildred (Sandy) Burger are pictured in 1921 arriving in Yorkville following World War I. They had been married in New York after Hale's discharge from the U.S. Navy. Mildred had been a designer of magazine covers for *Cosmopolitan* in New York and was a talented musician and artist. Yorkville must have been a shock for this young bride who had been born and reared in New York.

Georgia Burger is enjoying the sunshine on the porch of the Yorkville Elementary School around 1915. The school was located near the Yorkville Methodist Church. It was later disbanded and the children from this area were transported to Boonville. The building was torn down, and the lumber was used to build an additional room on the Anderson Valley Elementary School in Boonville (the present senior center).

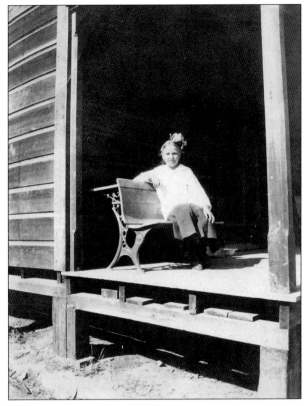

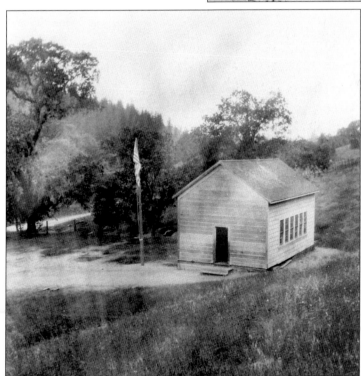

Gaskill School is shown here as it appeared in 1926 and was located south of Yorkville on Highway 128. The school was closed due to lack of attendance and students were transported to Boonville. The school building is still standing on property owned by Stanley Johnson, a former pupil.

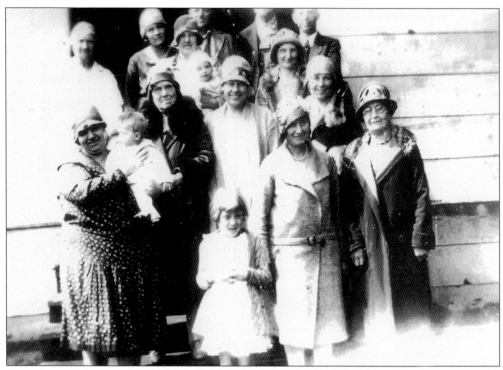

This photograph was taken in front of the Yorkville Methodist Church in 1929. Later that same year, it was torn down and the lumber was used to build a parsonage next to the Methodist church in Boonville. Many lamented with the phrase, "First they took our school, then our church." Pictured here are Ethel Hiatt and her baby, Catherine Nobles, Martha Hibbard, Martha Hibbard, Ida Nobles, Hazel Nobles, unidentified, Emily Presley and baby, Frieda Hibbard, Willie Ornbaun, unidentified, Raymond Ornbaun, unidentified, and Vernon Presley.

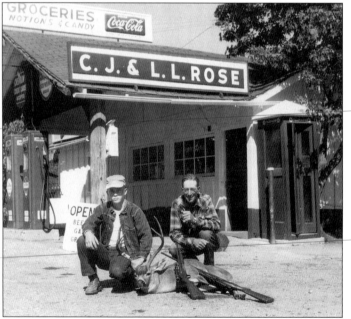

Allie Prather started the present store at Yorkville in the 1930s. After the 1937 flood, the post office was added. The store has had several owners over the years, including Mrs. Prather, Emmabelle Witherell, Wes Hulbert, Claude and Lou Rose, Leo and Barbara Marcott, and Debbie Johnson. It is obvious that Claude Rose and his young friend in the photograph had a very successful hunt. Claude was a popular storyteller and trapper and his store stocked everything from gasoline to groceries.

Seven

BOONT: THE CAPITAL

Brothers Henry and Isaac Beeson and their stepbrother William Anderson were probably the first white men to see Anderson Valley. In the fall of 1851, they started from Lake County to explore and hunt. They wounded an elk and, following its track, came out on the rocky point southeast of where Boonville now stands. They hurried back to tell their family about the area and reportedly their first attempt to settle was thwarted by Indians. Yet in the spring of 1852, they succeeded, building a home and raising horses and hogs. Mrs. Anderson died in 1857 and soon her husband sold his property to Joseph Rawles and left the valley. Their sons, Isaac and Henry Beeson, spent most of their lives in the area. Henry was an expert saddle maker, reputed to have made the easiest riding range saddles in the community, known as "Beeson Trees." His final ranch in the valley, known as the "Old Beeson Place," was where the forestry department is today. The Bear Flag continues to fly over the site where one of the original "bear flaggers" lived for 20 years until his death in 1914. Isaac Beeson never married and is remembered by some for his interest in church affairs. It is said that Isaac, who died in 1899, never missed a Sunday at church.

Boonville had two earlier names. First known as The Corners, it was located at the corner of Highways 253 and 128. In 1862, John Burgot built a hotel there, known as Anderson House. By 1864, there was also a blacksmith shop and a general store.

In the early 1860s, Alonzo Kendall opened a hotel where the present town of Boonville stands and called it Kendall City. Levi Strauss, the maker of Levi jeans, came from the gold fields and built a store near the hotel. He later sold the store to W. W. Boone (Daniel's cousin), and he changed the name to Booneville. Over time, the "e" was dropped and Boonville became Anderson Valley's largest commercial center.

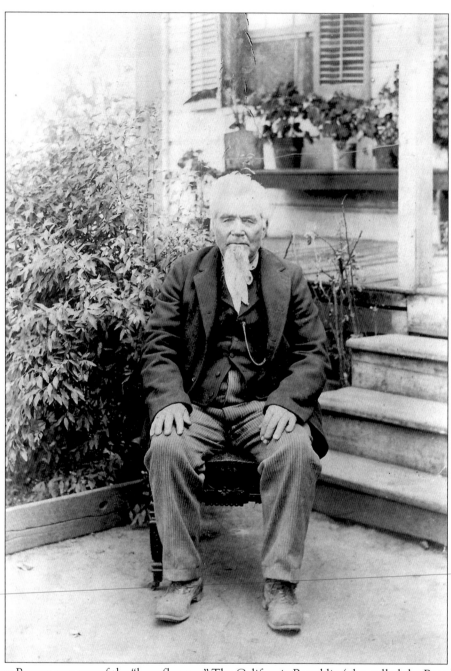

Henry Beeson was one of the "bear flaggers." The California Republic (also called the Bear Flag Republic) was created as the by-product of increasing tensions between the United States and Mexico. On June 10, 1846, John C. Fremont and his men went to Sonoma, knocked on General Vallejo's door, and declared independence from Mexico. They were called the "bear flaggers" because they raised a flag in the courtyard of Sonoma, which had a grizzly bear emblem. When the Mexican-American War began, the "bear flaggers" joined the war effort. A significant legacy of the California Republic is the State of California's adoption of the flag, which has a grizzly bear and the words "California Republic" near the bottom.

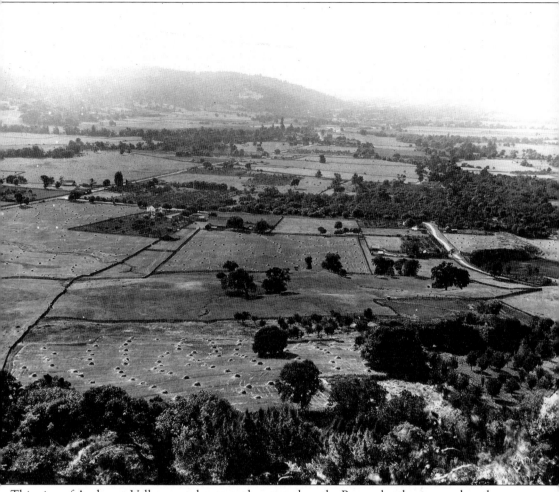

This view of Anderson Valley was taken near the same place the Beeson brothers were when they first saw Anderson Valley. It isn't hard to understand why they were so pleased with the spot, and after a few days they hurried back to Lake County to report that they had found a "big meadow, and it was like a garden of Eden." The roads shown are Highways 128 and 253.

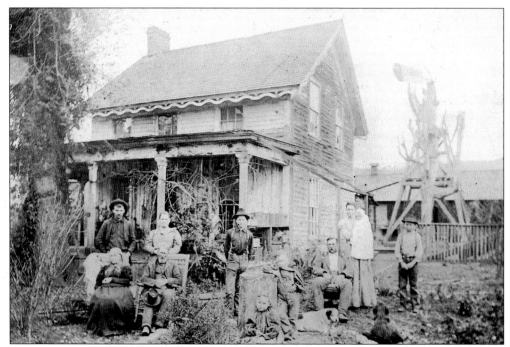

In the fall of 1852, J. D. Ball arrived in the valley. His journey began in New York and included stops in Wisconsin and Placerville, California. His home, shown here, was located near Con Creek. He created the first apple orchard in the valley and later constructed a building for his headquarters located across from the current Boonville Hotel.

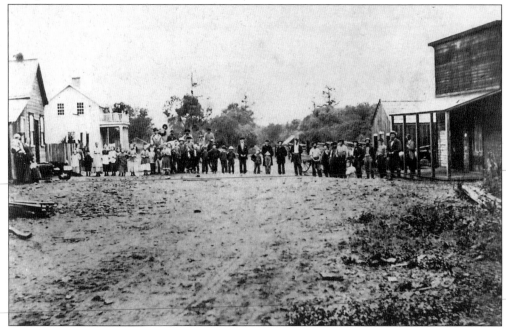

This early Boonville street scene was taken in the late 1860s or early 1870s. Alonza Kendall had built his hotel. Whether this was Kendall City or Boonville is unknown. It all depends on whether or not Boone owned the store when this picture was taken.

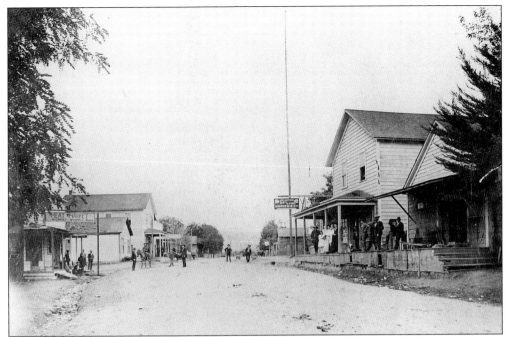

This Boonville street scene is dated October 23, 1909, and looks south, with the McGimsey and Whipple Meat Market on the left and J. T. Farrer's General Merchandise Store further down the street. Farrer was the seventh proprietor of the store. T. J. Rawles, George Brown, Woodward, Joe Rushing, Bolen Hiatt, and John Wallach previously owned this place of business. These names are a good representative of the early valley settlers. Across the street is Joe Antrim's Dry Goods and Groceries.

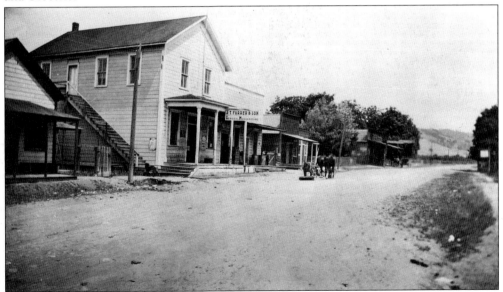

The stairs going up the side of the J. T. Farrer General Merchandise Store went to a dance hall, which was in use for a long time. Finally, it began to sway during dances and was closed. Walter and Beth Tuttle, who still reside in the valley, met at the dance hall. Donna Reilly, a valley resident, learned to dance there.

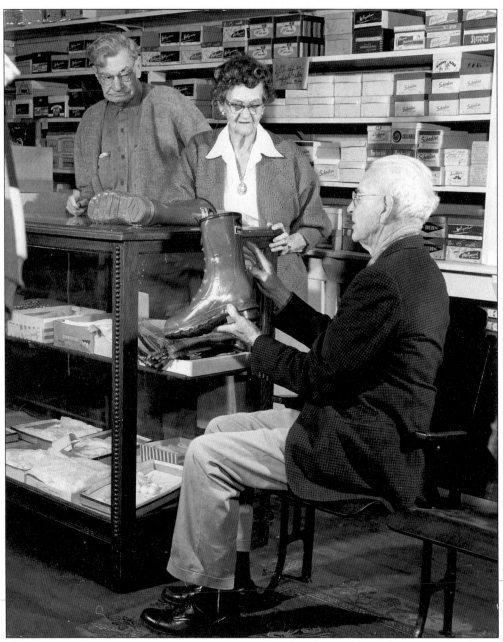

From the turn of the century to the mid-1950s, the people of Anderson Valley shopped at the J. T. Farrer General Merchandise Store. J. T. and Florence, shown here, made adjustments over the years, continually changing to meet the needs of the valley residents. During the boom years, a room was added as a women's apparel shop. When automobiles were becoming more common, they added a gas station, and it was later changed to a feed store. Eileen Pronsolino remembers their scales serving dual purposes, weighing both merchandise and the valley babies.

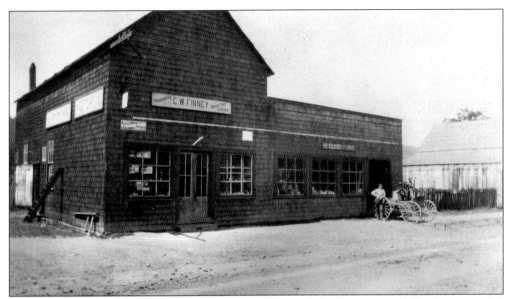

Charlie Finney was called "nickel-dime" Finney, as he priced everything, even dollar items, a nickel and a dime more. Charlie was the fourth proprietor of this shop as John McGimsey, Quorley, and Claude Johnson preceded him. As shown in 1915, Charlie's shop was a hardware and sporting goods store, and machine shop. Charlie had a great love of guns and could make almost any part needed for repairs. He had a place behind the shop to sight guns.

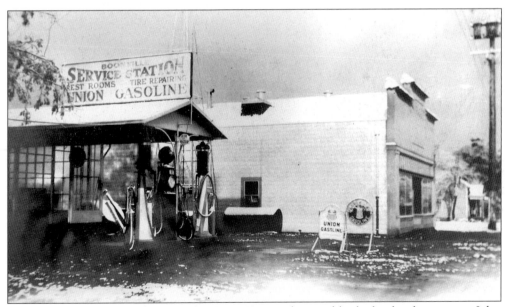

In 1918, Albert Ferrell tore down the C. W. Finney shop and built this hardware store. John Rossi and his son purchased the store from Albert in 1945 and Emil Rossi and Sons continue to operate the hardware today. While no longer a gas station, the Boonville Service Station is still a part of Boonville's commercial center.

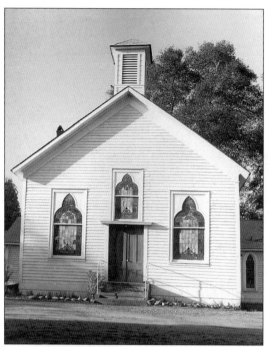

The Methodist Church South was dedicated in 1873 on land donated by John McAbee. Pastors were hard to come by, so at various times the church was connected with Cuffey's Cove, Navarro Ridge, and Cloverdale (in 1882). A parsonage was added in 1927, using lumber from the Yorkville Methodist Church. The stained-glass windows were brought around the Horn to Oakland in the late 1920s. This beautiful old building is still the church home of many valley residents.

During the early settlement days travel was difficult, so one-room schoolhouses were built throughout the valley. The Peachland School, *c.* 1925, was located about five miles east of Highway 128, between Boonville and Philo, with Mr. Carlson as the teacher. Beth Willis Tuttle, in the front row wearing the white dress, is the only identifiable student in the photograph.

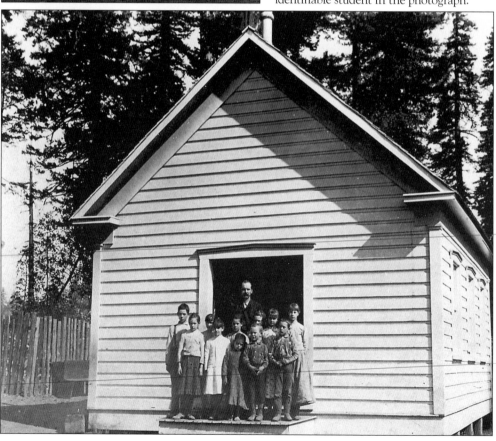

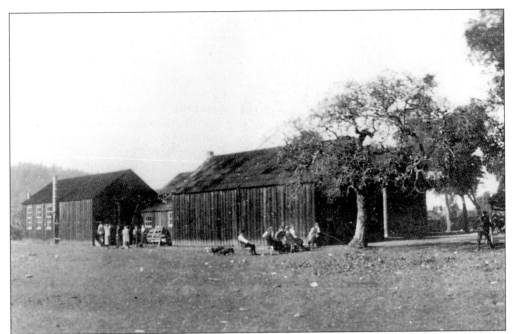

The first high school in Anderson Valley is shown in the left center. It was started in 1912 with one principal/teacher giving instruction to all students, with a four-year curriculum in a single classroom in a small wooden building; an additional classroom was added each year until there were five. The school was located near Con Creek and continued as the high school until 1921.

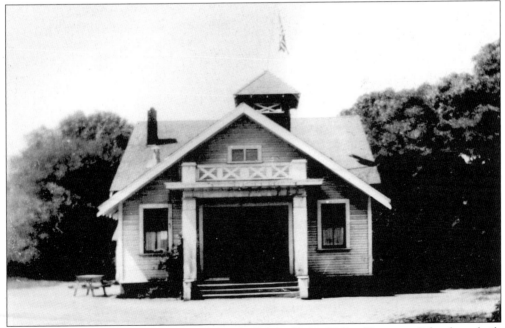

As the valley grew, schools were consolidated. The Anderson Valley Grammar School was built in Boonville using lumber from the Yorkville School. Today this building serves the community as the senior center and legion hall.

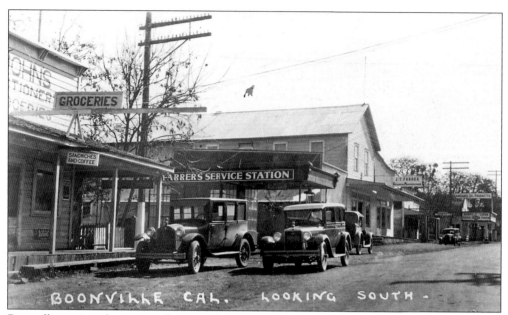

Boonville continued to grow as shown in this street scene, taken in the early 1930s. J. T. Farrer added a service station, and Standard Oil products were for sale down the street at the Boonville Lodge. This shows that the lodge serviced automobiles before it serviced valley residents as a bar.

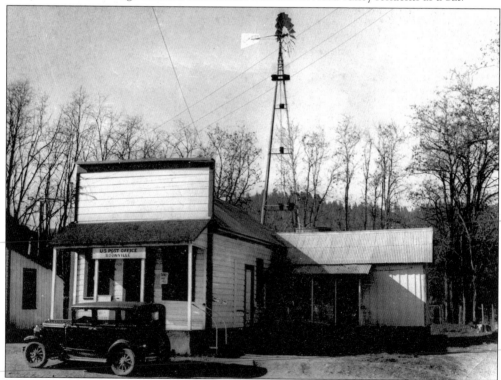

The post office was located on the west end of town before it was later moved to Tindall's Market. As the valley grew, the post office again needed a location of its own, resulting in the construction of the current post office.

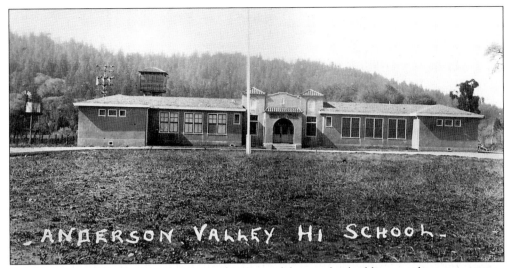

In 1922, a new high school was constructed in front of the wooden buildings on the same property as the old school. The gymnasium/auditorium came first, as basketball was an important part of life in the community. The gym was completed in time for graduation and classes began the following fall. This continued as the Anderson Valley High School until 1958. The new school, built that year, is still the home of the Anderson Valley Panthers.

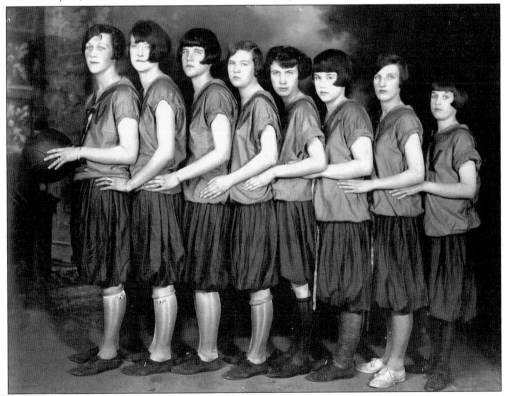

Sports have always been an important part of Anderson Valley schools as shown in this photograph of the 1924–1925 girls' basketball team. Pictured here are Velma Peterson, Daisy Peterson, Ina Peterson, Thelma Farrer, Maude Stites, Marguerite McAbee, Bernice Zill, and Vivian Hutsell.

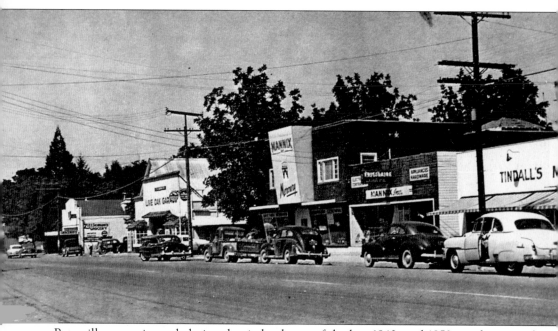

Boonville was at its peak during the timber boom of the late 1940s and 1950s, as shown in this 1940s street scene. In just this section of town, there were two grocery stores, Zittlemans and Tindalls. The Live Oak Garage serviced the valley automobiles and the Mannix building served as a ford dealership and a hardware and appliance store. Homer Mannix owned all of the businesses housed in the building. Later it was the location of the justice court, where Judge Homer Mannix presided. His wife, Beatrice, had a beauty shop next door. Homer also started the local paper, the *Anderson Valley Advertiser.*

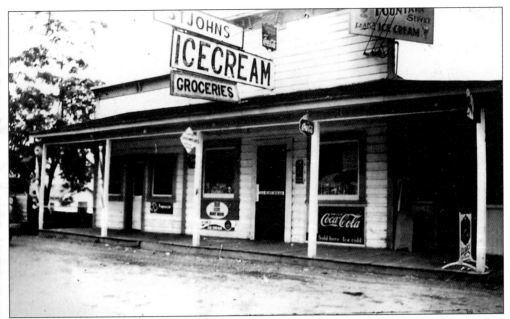

In the 1930s, St. John's was added on the north end of town. Sadie St. John sold groceries and operated the restaurant and ice cream shop, which also sold candy. Mrs. St. John made most of her own candy and its excellence was well known. Bill St. John had a barbershop and shoe repair shop.

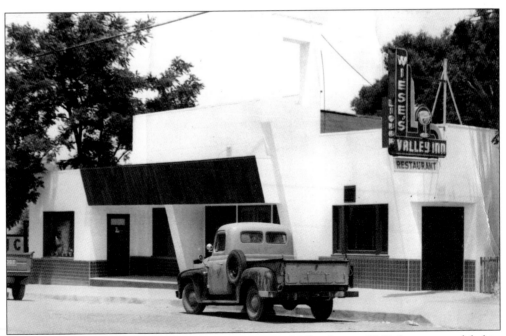

St. Johns was sold to the Wieses and became Wiese's Valley Inn in 1940. It was remodeled in 1954, taking on the modern look shown in this photograph. Wiese's was a restaurant, fountain shop, and bar. In the 1940s and 1950s, the fountain shop was the teenage hangout that had great french fries. It later burned down, leaving a gap on Boonville's main street.

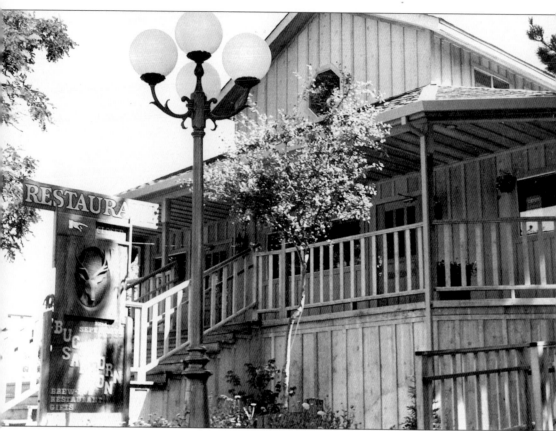

On December 26, 1987, the Anderson Valley Brewing Company filled the hole left vacant when Weise's burned down. They began brewing in the basement of their new Buckhorn Saloon. Their brewing system had a capacity of 10 barrels, or 310 gallons per batch. Bottling was done by hand, using champagne bottles. With the purchase of a 1946 Liquid Carbonic soda-bottling machine, bottling capabilities greatly improved and "Boonville Beer" was growing. In October 1995, they broke ground for a new facility located on the corner of Highways 128 and 253. The project included a brew house, with two copper Huppman systems purchased from two defunct breweries in Germany, a gift store, and tasting room.

Eight

POLEEKO

The town of Philo has had a name and a post office since June 18, 1888, thanks to a man named Cornelius Philo. He learned of the area from his brother William, who settled there in 1855. Cornelius, a blacksmith, wagon maker, carpenter, and bricklayer, acquired 160 acres near the town known now as Philo, and built a home and planted an orchard. Through his efforts, the post office began operating, the town was named, and Indian Creek School District was formed, and he dedicated land for the Philo Methodist Church. His home is still in use as the Philo Pottery Inn.

Before Philo's founding, Christine was the major commercial center in the lower end of the valley. Founders Mr. and Mrs. John Gschwend, natives of Switzerland who settled in 1855, named the town after their daughter, the first Caucasian child born in Anderson Valley. Six other Swiss families arrived with them: the Guntlys, Conrads, Schneiders, Kirrys, Hausemans, and the Gossmans. After constructing a home, John Gschwend built a sawmill near Mill Creek. In 1865, he converted it to a gristmill. In search of markets for his timber, he built the road to Ukiah, which was a toll road. He also opened the first wagon road to the coast by way of Navarro Ridge. A spur of the railroad that ran between Albion and Navarro ran to Christine Landing. The Wendling mill stacked lumber there, allowing it to dry while awaiting shipment.

Over time, the east side of the road became Guntlyville, owned by Andrew and Mary Guntly. Christine and Guntlyville were stage stops with mail service. Mr. Guntly ran the Guntlyville Post Office and Mrs. Guntly ran the Guntlyville Inn. Their son Ed eventually purchased the old homestead and other adjoining properties, accumulating 1,581 acres. He was a successful rancher who, among other things, supplied meat to surrounding settlements. Later, this ranch was split, with a portion of it becoming the area we now know as Holmes Ranch.

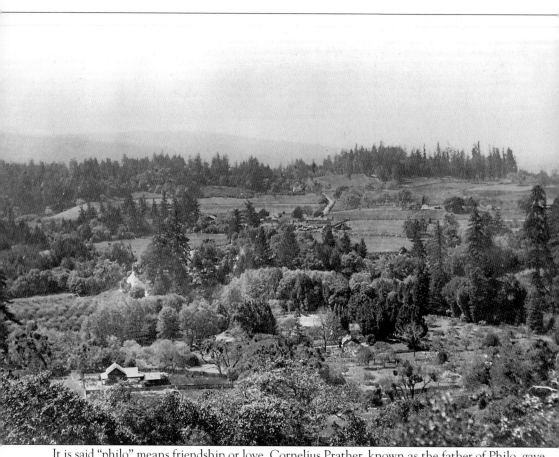

It is said "philo" means friendship or love. Cornelius Prather, known as the father of Philo, gave the name to this beautiful area after his favorite girl cousin, Philomena. This picture, a view of Philo looking north from near the Ruddock Cemetery, was taken in 1913.

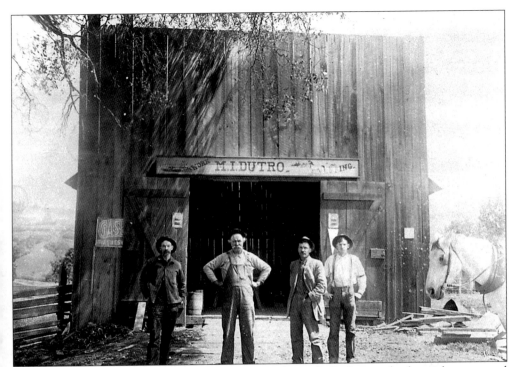

The M. L. Dutro Blacksmith Shop sat under a spreading oak. Dad was indeed a mighty man and "Kid" Dutro was the one who shod big-footed horses of the teams as well as saddle and buggy horses. The shop was a meeting place for those who had a few minutes to spare. Pictured here are Dow Whipple, Mart Dutro, Earl Prather, and Neil Chipman.

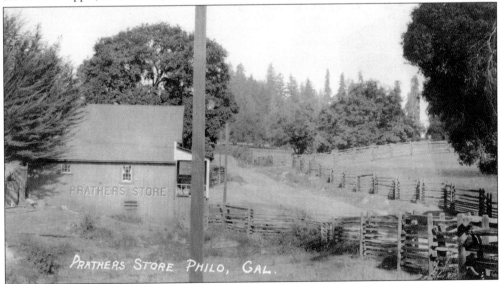

Across a little bridge from the blacksmith shop was John L. Prather's store, which offered groceries in bulk. Cheese was available in large round wheels, which could be cut to any size. Overalls, work shirts, coal oil in five gallon cans, sewing needles, frying pans, butter churns, rifle shells, a few guns, and Star tobacco were all in stock at the Prather Store. Later they closed their store and moved to Yorkville.

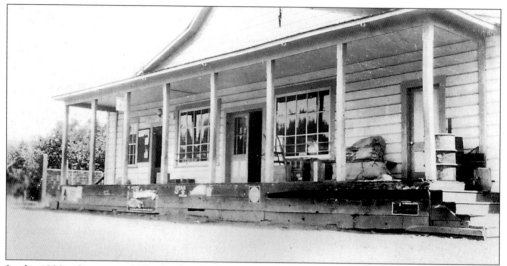

In the 1920s, George and Elizabeth Johnson opened a mercantile store in Philo, which was their second store after the first burned down sometime between 1915 and 1918. The first door went into the post office, the next door was the main store door, then down the steps to the south a shed housed feed and grain. Gas pumps stood in front of the shed door. Lemon's Market has been serving the community from this same building for many years.

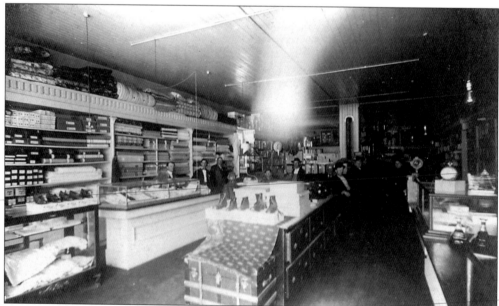

When entering the George Johnson Merchandise Store a person could see Mr. Johnson leaning on the counter near the cash register. Cheese and a big slab of bacon stood on the end of the counter, waiting to be cut. On the candy counter, Baby Ruths and Icy Flips sat in their square containers on stands, tempting all who came in. There was also a switchboard in the shoe room. Aunt Lizzie was the "central," switching calls as they came in to the Farmer's Line.

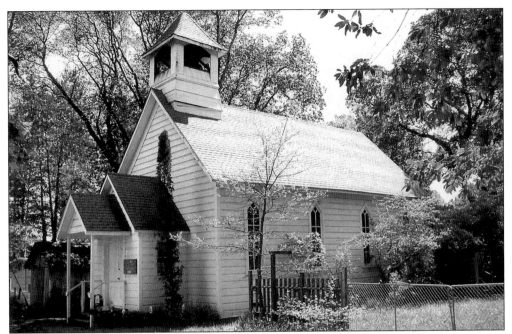

Cornelius Prather donated land for the first post office, school, and church in Philo. The church property was deeded with the stipulation that it would revert to his heirs if the building ever stopped being used for religious purposes. The community rallied and, with volunteer labor and donated materials, the church was built in 1891. The church bells still ring under the fine trees on the Prather land.

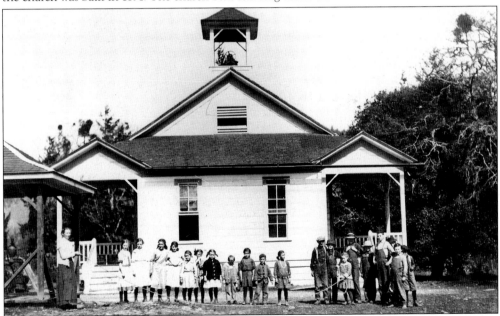

The first Philo School was built on Cornelius's land with no deed to it. Years later the noise of the children began to annoy him and he served notice that the school would have to move. He provided another site, which was a good location across the road. The Indian Creek School was built and served the area until unification happened in the valley. This photograph was taken in 1913. Mrs. Gussie Elder-Ruddock is the teacher holding the rope.

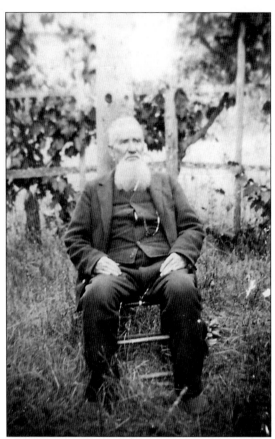

As a doctor, and a good one, John Treble "Doc" Brown was a godsend to Anderson Valley. His wife Elizabeth would ride on a pillion behind his saddle when a nurse was needed. A gifted and wonderful physician, he was also known for his quick temper. Many a patient experienced his irritability when they didn't follow his directions.

Doc Brown's home, shown here in 1893, is located just west of Philo. The ministers of the times looked forward to his meal invitations. His wife was a capable and pleasant hostess and following a wonderful meal, the men would sit in front of the fireplace and the fireworks would begin. They called it "wit sharpening." It remains as a valley home today.

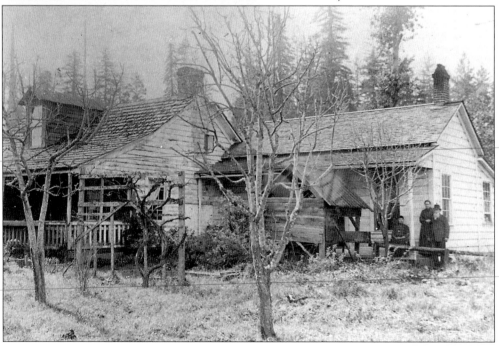

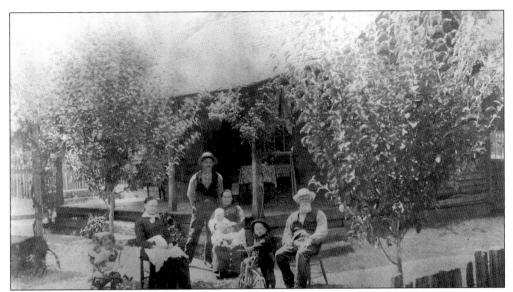

This was C. H. Clow's first valley home, pictured *c.* 1884. It was recorded in a 1922–1923 report from the Mendocino County Farm Bureau that "C. H. Clow gave a demonstration pruning of twelve pear trees, using long, modified, and short methods. Modified pruning was recommended. F. Rawles was the co-operator." The Clows can be found throughout valley history as mill owners, store owners, and ranchers. Pictured here, from left to right, are Bertha Clow, Eliza Clow, Reece Clow, Johanna Zimmerman Clow, Arnold Clow (on her lap), Henry Clow, and C. H. Clow.

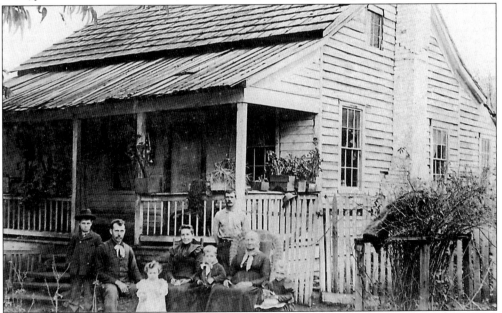

The Studebaker home (1903) was located at Christine Junction. While living in Sacramento, the family traded stock for a valley claim. Upon arrival in 1868, Mrs. Studebaker was disappointed with the small log cabin on the claim. In 1876, they bought part of the Nunn Ranch and built this home and planted apple trees. Studebaker descendents still farm these lands. Pictured here are Gilbert Price, Sumner Price, Ellis Price, Katie Studebaker Price, Clyde Price, Miller Studebaker, Nancy Studebaker, and Hazel Bennett.

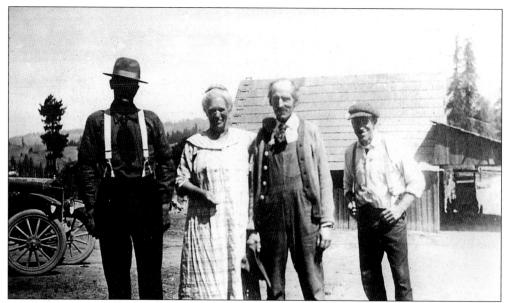

Mr. and Mrs. John Gschwend, shown here in 1925 with a friend and their son Walter, arrived in Anderson Valley in 1855. They were natives of Switzerland. Their daughter Christine was the first Caucasian child born in Anderson Valley. They settled in the lower end of the valley, naming their settlement after their daughter. Today their great, great granddaughter resides in the home they built. Pictured here are Fred Duffield, Julia Gschwend, John Gschwend II, and Walter Gschwend.

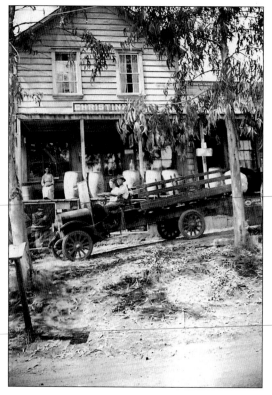

This is storekeeper Cecil Brown sitting in his truck in front of the Christine Store in 1920. The small settlement was the first in the valley. It was located about four miles south of Wendling, which today is known as Navarro.

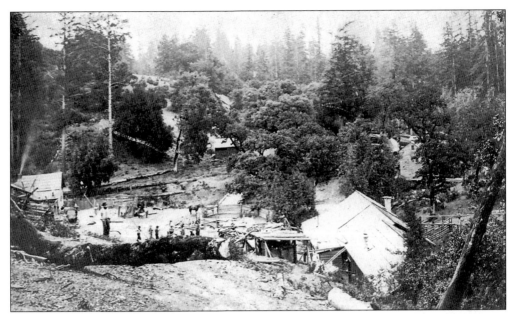

In 1856, John Gschwend built a sawmill near Mill Creek. When the mill stopped operating, Gschwend had 20-million board feet of lumber ready for local consumption. In 1864, the sawmill was converted to a water-powered gristmill.

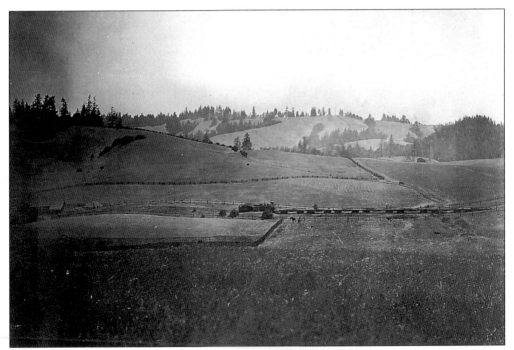

Christine Landing, shown here, was the end of the railroad line. This area, across from the town of Christine, was developed as a railroad stop for the logging trains in the area. They hauled lumber from the Wendling Mill and stacked it in the open ground at Christine Landing to dry.

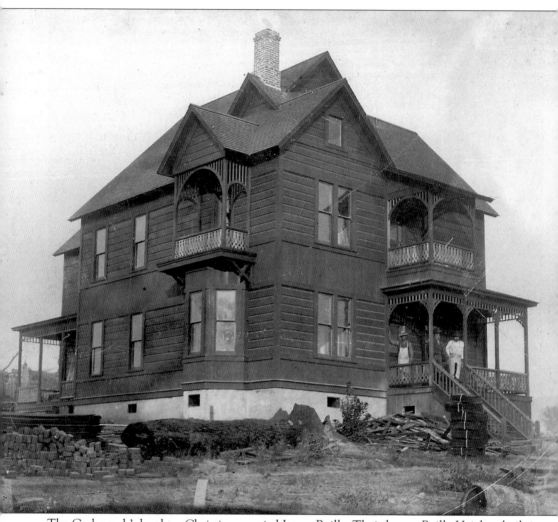

The Gschwends' daughter Christine married James Reilly. Their home, Reilly Heights, built in 1895–1896, was under construction in this picture. The lumber used for the home was hauled by team from the mill at the mouth of the Navarro, over Navarro Ridge Road. Their home was built by Henry Wightman, who also constructed two other valley landmarks. Reilly Heights is still in the family for which it was built.

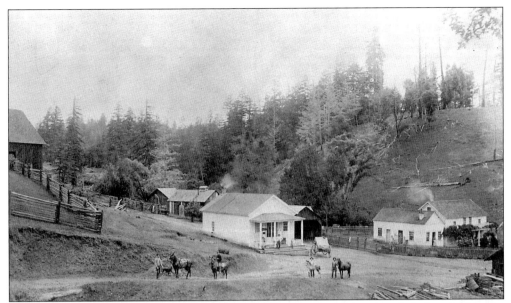

The first Gschwend settlement later became Guntlyville. Shown here in 1895, Guntlyville was located on Mill Creek. When Mr. Gschwend built the sawmill, Mrs. Guntly constructed a boarding room at Guntlyville for the mill workers. Mr. Guntly constructed a distillery and brewery, which ran until the advent of the bonding law, approximately 1870. The Guntlys built a store and began an accommodation banking service.

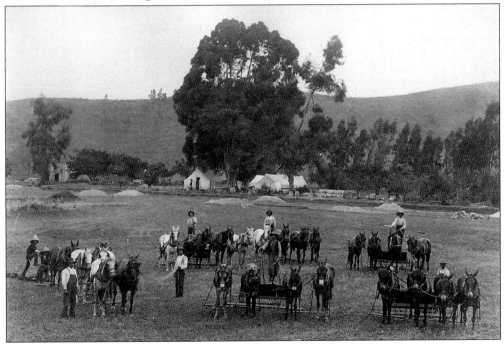

This railroad building crew was headquartered on the Guntly Ranch; note the piles of gravel in the background. The mule teams are pulling Fresnos, which were used to cut the land for the tracks. The ranch was sold by the Guntly family in 1955, changed ownership several times, and was finally established as the Holmes Ranch Subdivision in 1972.

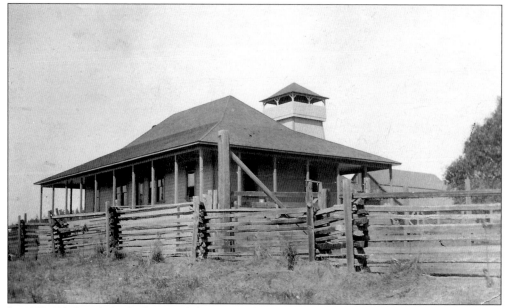

In 1913, Ed Guntly built this ranch home on the ranch. It was a large, one-story house with a basement. In back there was a large grove of live oak trees. In the front of the house was a huge white oak tree where Andrew Guntly, Ed's father, camped when he first arrived in the valley. This home is now a part of Handley Cellars.

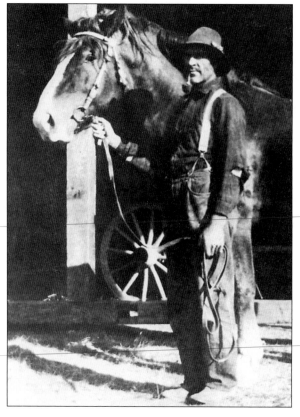

The Guntly Ranch ran cattle. During the early lumber boom days, they also oversaw a slaughterhouse that provided beef to the mill camps in Wendling and Hop Flat. Ed Guntly is shown here with his breeding stud, Coach.

Nine

ITEVILLE

G. X. Wendling built the Wendling Redwood Shingle Mill in 1902. Soon after the mill was completed, he made an agreement with the Albion and Southeastern to extend their railroad to his mill. The railroad was completed in September 1905. Earlier that year, A. G. Stearns purchased the Wendling Redwood Shingle Company. In 1908, Sterns made an agreement with Northwestern Pacific Railroad to extend their track from Wendling to Christine Landing (three and a half miles). Known as the Floodgate Extension, this track crossed ravines and rivers, and required 100 men and 80 mule teams to build.

In 1905, the town of Wendling was platted by the Wendling Springs Company. P. E. Lamar surveyed it, and in September 1905, streets were named and parcels readied for sale. W. T. Garrett and Company Real Estate sold the lots, which extended from Horse Haven Ranch to the juncture of Highway 128 and the Navarro Dump Road.

In 1914, The Navarro Lumber Company purchased the Sterns Lumber Company. The name of the mill changed with each owner. Eventually, the town of Navarro and the Navarro Mill became just Navarro. This was confusing because Capt. Charles Fletcher had settled at the mouth of the Navarro River in 1849, naming that settlement and the river Navarro. To rectify the confusion, the town of Wendling was officially changed to Navarro. The settlement at the mouth became Old Navarro, or Navarro Ridge, and later Navarro-By-The Sea.

In August 1920, the Albion Lumber Company purchased the Navarro Lumber Company for $247,750. This included the railroad, rolling stock, sawmill, hotel, lodging house, shops, and cookhouses—or "Mill Town." In 1922, the railroad was extended another three and a half miles down Perry Gulch.

While the railroad was built to haul lumber, it was soon used for hauling other products and passengers. On May 17, 1908, the first "Excursion Picnic Train" traveled from Albion to Wendling, and Dago Town became the entertainment center of Wendling. Hotels, restaurants, picnics, and entertainment gave the hard-working families a welcome outlet.

Eventually, the demand for lumber stopped; the mills and rails were rusting away. In 1937, the railroad and parts of the mill were sold to Hyman-Michaels as iron scrap, and the Wendling/Navarro boom ended.

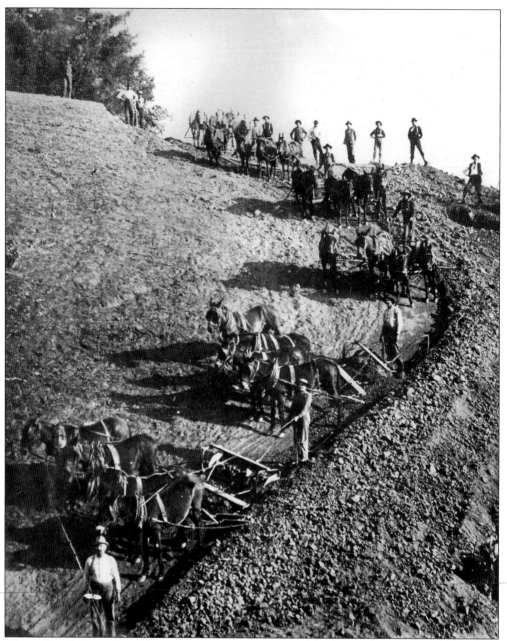

This railroad crew is building the Floodgate extension (1909–1910). The earth was moved by a Fresno Scraper, which was pulled by a four-mule team. The scraper was controlled by a long handle extending from the back and for digging it was raised up slightly. When pushed down, the scraper carried the dirt. To dump the load, the handle was lifted all the way up, causing the scraper to rotate forward and dump the dirt.

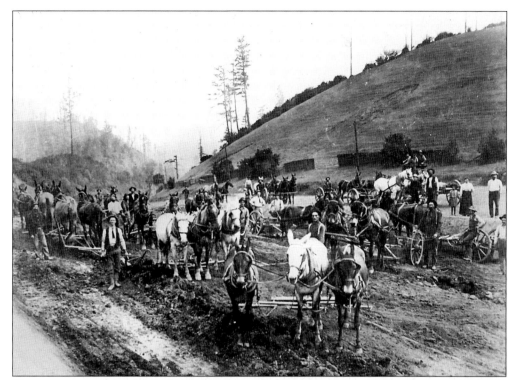

The crew continues on down the trail, building the extension. It took over 100 men and 80 mule teams to build the three-and-a-half-mile Floodgate extension.

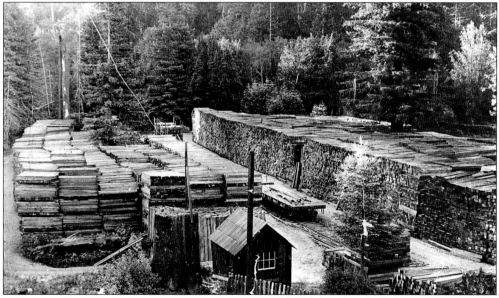

These railroad ties were stockpiled four miles north of Wendling in this 1926 photograph. There were over 118,000 ties, but the market was slow and they were unable to sell the ties. The short, flat cars were pulled up the gulches by horses or a steam donkey, loaded with ties, and returned by gravity to this location. When sold, they were hauled by horse and wagon to a railhead, and transported to Albion by train and loaded on a schooner.

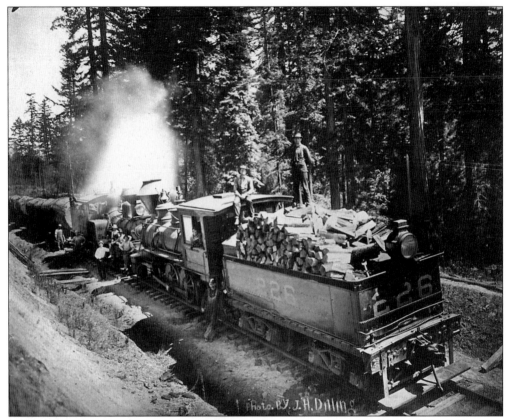

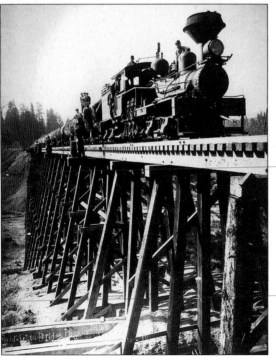

The Albion No. 226 and No. 2 Shay were passing near Floodgate when this picture was taken in 1908. This train carried logs and lumber from Sterns Mill in Wendling to Albion. Oscar Newman was the engineer.

The Wendling Shay No. 2 is crossing the Floodgate Trestle on July 23, 1910. The trains traveled terrain that had many gulches and rivers, making trestles a common part of the railroad. They were challenging during the building of the railroads.

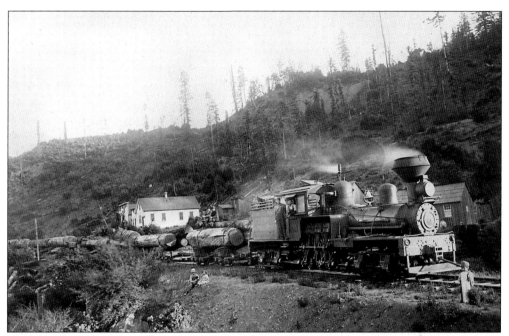

The Wendling Shay Engine No. 2 pulls into the mill with a load of logs in 1910, with Clarence Stout as the engineer. Trains that transported logs used the Shay Engine. It had three cylinders, which drove a long drive shaft to a gear box and then to the wheels, making it a more powerful engine. It also had small wheels, giving it more traction. Children often came to watch the train pass.

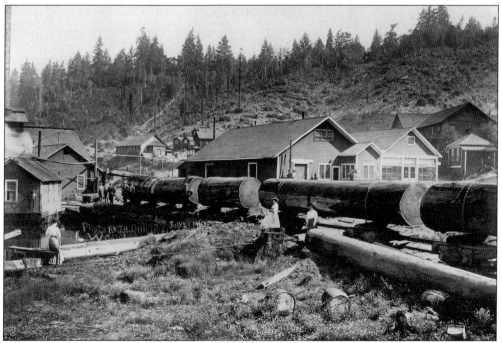

The train is stopped at the Sterns Mill in 1910. The building to the rear and right of the train housed the Company Store and Post Office. The large building in the back right was the dance hall, also used as a show house. Notice the ladies, who are dressed in their finery.

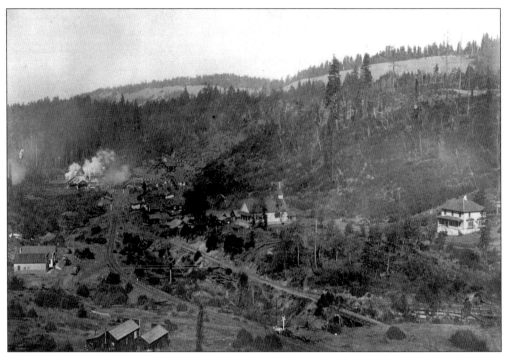

This 1915 overview of Wendling shows Mill Town and the Sterns Mill is identifiable by the smoke stack. The small building above the fork was the jail and Laurel School is the large center building above the road. The large, two-story home on the far right was the home of A. G. Sterns. The school and home are still standing today.

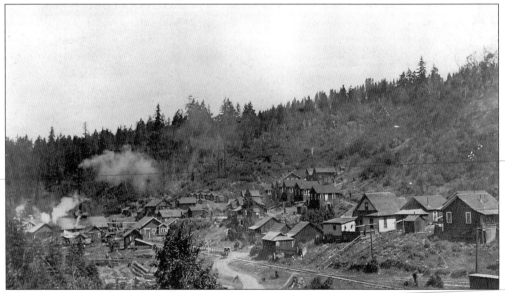

This is a close-up of Wendling Mill Town and the mill is identifiable by the smoke stack. The cookhouse, with rooms above for the crew, was located near the smoke stack. A hotel and post office were located next to the cookhouse. The company store, offices, and warehouse were next to the hotel. Above the mill there was a small cluster of single men's cabins and family houses. A dance hall and movie house sat above the lumber sorting yards.

The boiler room for the mill is being built in 1904 in this photograph. The mill was steam-powered and water was obtained from springs via tunnels that were dug into the hillside, the longest of which was about 150 feet. These tunnels provide water to some Navarro residents today. Wood waste was used to fire the steam furnace.

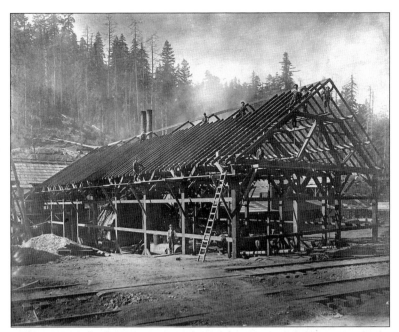

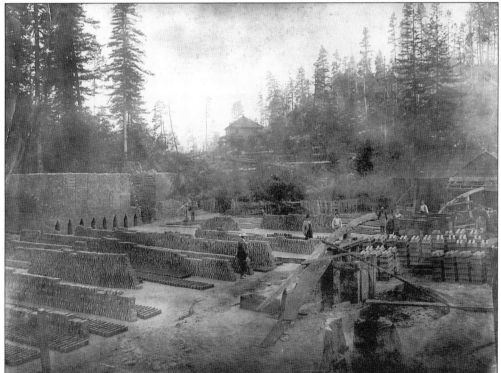

The bricks manufactured in this brickyard were used to construct the mill furnace; the kiln is shown in the far left center and the molds are shown on the far right. Haywood Scott, wearing the white hat, was the plant foreman. The clay for the bricks was excavated from a nearby hillside. The brickyard was located where the Navarro Store still stands today. The A. G. Stearns home can be seen in the background.

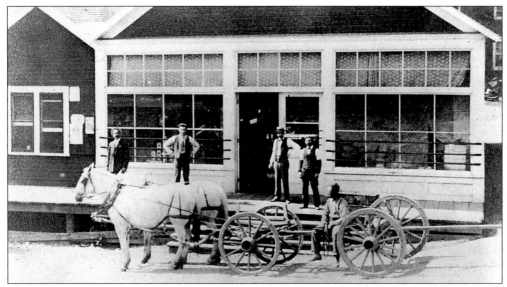

This was the Wendling Store, which was also the Company Store; the Sterns Lumber Company office is left of the store. The wagon in front of the store was equipped to haul lumber and the bunks at the front and back and the reach extending beyond the back axel could be adjusted for different lengths of lumber. In February 1908, a second store was built. After the mill closed, another store was constructed, which today is known as the Navarro Store.

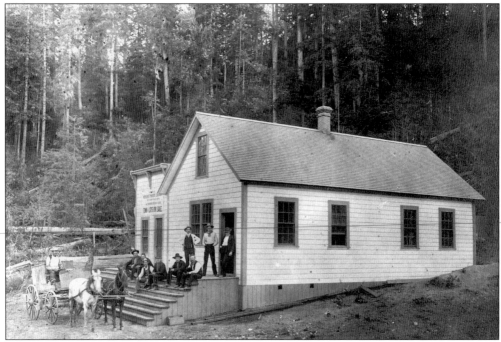

In 1905, the town of Wendling was laid out on plat maps as a subdivision, with P. E. Lamar doing the surveying. In September 1905, W. T. Garrett and Company Real Estate, doing business out of the building that says "Town Lots for Sale," began selling the lots. The F. Estill meat wagon delivered fresh meat to stores, hotels, and individual ranchers. Ernest Pardini later purchased the large building from Bob Tison and today it is known as the Ice House.

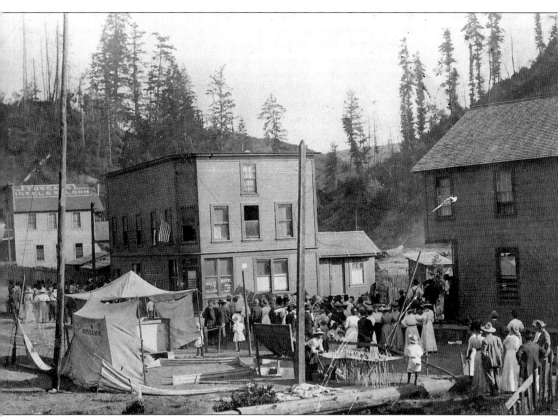

Southeast of the mill was a community of hotels and restaurants, called "Dago Town," pictured here in 1906. At the very far left of the photograph, a portion of the Twin Hotel can be seen. Next door is the Toscano Hotel, owned and operated in its early days by the Pasero family. The third hotel, seen in the center of the photograph, is the Hotel D'Italia. The Stearns Lumber Company constructed this building, intending to use it as a hospital for their mill workers, but it never operated in this capacity. Alciede Bacci, of Vinegar Hill, converted it to a restaurant, bar, and hotel. In 1907, Joe and Sabatine (Mama) Pardini purchased it and the name changed to Pardini's Hotel. Mama and her sister Beppa provided the valley with sumptuous dinners for over 50 years. Later it again underwent extensive remodeling, becoming the Navarro Inn, which burned down in 1974. To the far right is the Ainsley Hotel. The group in the picture was gathered for a Fourth of July celebration.

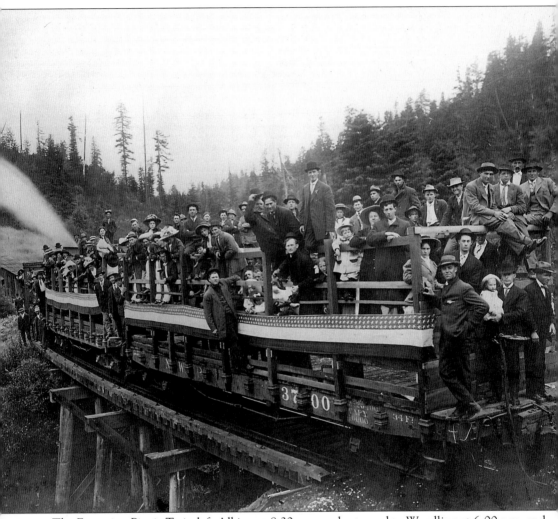

The Excursion Picnic Train left Albion at 8:30 a.m. and returned to Wendling at 6:00 p.m. and the fare was $1. Local residents used it for days of fun on the coast and city dwellers used it to get to the valley. Men from the city, who had just returned from a steelhead fishing trip on the Navarro, could be seen strolling through the dining room of Pardini's Hotel, highballs in hand, resplendent in hip boots on their way to their hotel rooms.